What? Not another book about relationships! Considering that you can buy just about anything today for any need, you still "can't buy me love" as The Beatles once sang. Herein is the basis for this book – the need to love and be loved. Where does it come from and how can it be kept going? "One minute we're fine, the next our partnership is nearly at breaking point" you might groan.

This is a book for anyone wanting an enduring relationship, whether married or not. It is filled with real life scenarios, sound practical advice and interactive things to do – with one goal in mind – to enrich our relationships so that they grow into life-long loving partnerships.

From the publisher.

Hang on... I need to say SOMETHING!

Gillian Warren

Illustrations by

Jacky Fleming

Gazelle Books

Harpenden, Herts AL5 4SE.
England.

First published 1997
by Gazelle Books, Station Road, Harpenden, Herts, AL5 4SE
England, UK.

ISBN 1 899746 09 9

British Library Cataloging in Publication Data.
A record for this book is available from the British Library.

Designed and Produced in England for
GAZELLE BOOKS
by Nuprint Ltd, Station Road, Harpenden, Herts AL5 4SE.

Contents

Foreword

I was privileged to read this sensitive, intelligent book in manuscript form. As I turned the pages I kept wishing that I could send different chapters to various friends.

And there were chapters I thought I should post to myself – with *Priority* written on the envelope! Here is wisdom from which everyone should benefit.

I was reminded of a week when I was admitted to the intensive care unit of a large hospital 200 miles from home. My wife was encouraged by the dozens of get well cards which were brought to the ward each morning. Strangely, I didn't want to look at them. Afterwards, searching my heart for the reason, I guessed it was because I hated to think that anyone knew I was ill. I'd always been well, able to cope, fit for all daily life demanded. I wanted to keep my problem a secret, to keep up the image and not lose face.

Foolish? Absolutely. Yet many couples do this when an apparently happy partnership threatens to break down. Storms rage inside the home but understandably the couple attempts to give the impression of a contented stable couple. If, through lack of help and counselling, a separation or divorce follows, it proves a devatating blow to their family friends.

Because of our imperfections there is no completely perfect partnership. We should all acknowledge that our relationship together, whether new or long established, could be better. We take a giant step forward when we come to appreciate this. Suddenly we are open to receiving help and suggestions. This is where *Hang On . . . I Need To Say Something* is certain to be a catalyst for revitalising weary relationships and to give wisdom to those starting out in life intending to stay together.

I found it like an honest face to face chat with Gillian Warren, across the kitchen table over a cup of coffee, a kind of intimate sharing with one of the wisest of counsellors. She was actually answering my questions without my asking them! Here is a startlingly fascinating recipe for a happy partnership together.

Edward England
Crowborough, East Sussex

Introduction

This is not a manual on marriage. It's more like highlighting on a page of text. It's to draw attention to some areas where we could strengthen our relationships and give them a face-lift.

My husband and I got married in 1957. In those days there were no books giving you helpful hints for getting over the inevitable problems, or tips about love-making. One older lady warned us that it wouldn't be 'roses, roses, all the way', but we were too starry-eyed to believe her. We never imagined that the early months would involve huge adjustments, and a struggle to cope with our many differences. We found we needed lots of patience, and had to work hard to understand each other. We had to discover how to meet in the middle over all sorts of things that never cropped up till we lived together.

Michael trained at college to be a farmer. I was doing a degree and expecting to do further training for my career. But no one suggested that we train for the biggest career of all – marriage. In fact, in those days, such training hardly existed.

We spent an hour or so with the minister, discussing hymns and prayers, and that was it. We had a wonderful wedding in a country church, and later we climbed into a car and drove away into our future.

Everyone wished us well, as people do, but not a word of advice did they offer us. I was twenty. Michael was twenty-nine. We were madly in love, full of optimism, thrilled to be together at last, after two and a half years of waiting.

The time was winter. The flat where we began our married life was unheated except by a tiny wood fire that smoked. The kitchen measured about six feet by six feet, enough room to turn round, and I was useless at cooking. My early attempts often reduced me to tears. But my new, hungry farmer husband would be coming in for a meal, and he had to have something to eat. It was a good thing that we were so in love. Otherwise we might never have survived that first winter – the cold, and the awful food.

That was nearly forty years ago, and things are different, very different, for couples considering marriage today. But human nature hasn't changed. You have your dreams, just as we had ours. You may have pictured marriage as the answer to all your longings, the pot of gold at the end of the rainbow, an eternal romance! So did we. But sooner or later we all discover that the best things in life don't just fall into our laps: we have to work for them.

We found that out when we started a garden. Unless we worked at it, it soon became a wilderness of weeds and tall grass. It took about eight years and a lot of hard work before it really began to look settled. We had so much to learn. It took twenty-five years and a weekend marriage seminar before we began to talk about our sex life and what we both enjoyed. Just think of all those lost years! For ages we never talked about our feelings. Michael was one of the 'stiff upper lip brigade' – never show your feelings at any price. I came from a home where hugs and tears were rarely seen. Nevertheless, we were very happy, but there was still so much more ahead for us.

Through going to seminars and reading recommended books during those weekends, we began to give an evening a month to ourselves, to share how we felt, talk through the times we'd felt hurt, or had neglected or failed to respond to the other, or been a disappointment. We started talking about our deeper feelings, and we've grown closer and closer in the years we've been doing this. It's taken a long time because for the first twenty-five years we had no help at all.

That's why I wanted to write this book. I hope you haven't had to wait twenty-five years to find some hints about how to improve your relationship. Perhaps you're right at the beginning. That's just the time to pick up some 'hints for a contented life together'. Most of what you read here isn't new. You know it all, deep down inside, but it helps to see it in print and discover ways of putting it into practice.

I'm sure you want your partnership to be happy, and it can be. There's so much we can do to help our relationships to improve and flourish as the years go by. Remember it is a living, changing organism that needs plenty of nourishment and loving attention. Resolve to give it the time and input it deserves, and your efforts will be rewarded by increasing fulfilment.

And if, as you read this, you're thinking, 'Oh dear, mine's past that stage,' please read on. Many, many people think this, but by following some of these suggestions, your life together can thrive again.

We have two hydrangeas in large pots by our front door. They began to wilt in a severe drought. The leaves were curling up and drooping. They looked half dead...until Michael began to water them regularly. Then they perked up and began to look healthy and happy again. The same will happen to your partnership if you start to 'water' it regularly.

We've been married now for thirty-eight years. There have been wonderful times and tough times along the way, but at this stage one of our greatest joys, apart from our children, is the multitude of memories we share. Reminiscing is a great delight and makes us deeply thankful.

I couldn't wish anything more for you: a life-long partnership that grows and deepens, rides out the bumps and the storms, and is still there for you, your children and your grandchildren in the years to come. Whatever the world may say, there is no deeper satisfaction than a couple who are enjoying a life-long partnership together.

'Hang On – Can I Say Something?'

Nick and Jane had had a bad night. Baby Tom was teething and they were up four times. Now Nick was hastily swallowing his coffee before dashing off to work.

Jane was dreading the day. Joanna was due at playgroup by 9.30 am, but Tom wasn't really well enough to be taken in the pushchair. She had to do some cleaning. You could write your name in the dust everywhere. And she had a headache brewing.

'Nick,' she began, looking at him hopefully.

The coffee cup crashed into the saucer as Nick looked at his watch.

'Must dash,' he said. 'Traffic's so bad these days.' He gave Jane a quick peck on the cheek, grabbed his case and was gone.

Jane sat down on the stool, still warm where Nick had used it, and began to cry. She poured a lukewarm cup of coffee, held it between her hands and gulped mouthfuls, staring at the dirty kitchen floor. Then the baby cried. The dreaded day had begun.

Nick didn't understand. He didn't notice. He just rushed off to work, and she wanted to call after him, 'Hang on – I want to say something!' But she knew the answer would come back: 'Can't stop now – we'll talk later!'

'Later?' When would 'later' be? When he came home it was the garden, or the car, or the telly, or a noisy meal with the children, or phone calls to do with work. But never a time when they sat down together to talk about themselves. Hot tears burst out of her eyes and ran down her cheeks. She tore off a piece of kitchen roll and mopped her face.

'Where are you, Nick?' she cried in her heart. 'I love you. I need you. I want to talk to you. Please hang on a minute.'

Have you ever felt like Jane? Do you know how your partner is feeling about life right now? Did you know that your husband was in daily fear of losing his job since a new boss took over?

Why is it so hard to keep in touch once we're married with a family? It's as if someone has cut the telephone line and we don't know why and can't get it mended – or can we?

Kevin was late home from work again. When he came in, Margaret thought he smelt slightly of scent or powder. He only gave her a quick kiss, then changed into gardening gear and began to dig the new border.

Margaret was very quiet over supper. She was worried and upset. As soon as the meal was over she went upstairs for a bath and got into bed. Kevin wondered what was the matter. Why was she so quiet? Why the early bed? He went up and sat on the bed beside her, found her hand under the duvet and held it in his.

'What's the matter, love? Are you upset about something?'

Margaret lay there and looked at him. He could see the anxiety and hurt in her eyes.

'Have I done something? Is it my fault?' he asked.

Then it all came spilling out. The smell of powder, the too-quick kiss, the haste to get into the garden, the fear that....

Kevin pulled Margaret close and stroked her hair. Then he explained that there was a girl at work whose boyfriend had just walked out. She was sobbing and Kevin had comforted her. As for the garden, he'd genuinely wanted to get the digging done.

'I'm so sorry not to have greeted you properly. Please forgive me. I just wasn't thinking.'

They had a long hug and the hurt was healed.

Have you got something you're longing to say to your partner? Even perhaps an accumulating file of things? When are you going to talk them through? When can you make a date together?

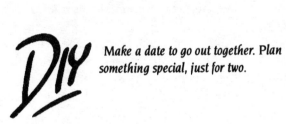 *Make a date to go out together. Plan something special, just for two.*

'Hang On – Don't Hang Up!'

Hurry, hurry. Rush and dash. 'Must go!' 'Have to run now!' 'Can't stop!' 'No time to talk!' Like a train tearing through the countryside, we're tearing through the weeks and months of our life. The train dashes through every station, never stopping, faster and faster – and no one pulls the communication cord, the emergency stop.

If we're not talking to each other, then it's an emergency. We need to pull that cord – NOW! Stop the hectic whirl of the week and start relating again – talking and listening to each other. How can we find the time? Because no time, no talk. It's that simple.

When would be a possible moment? After the evening meal, without the TV on? Sunday afternoon during a walk? During a Saturday morning lie-in? Or last thing at night if you're not too tired? Perhaps over a drink at the pub? Or eating a Chinese take-away or fish and chips in the park?

N.B. Dates we've agreed together must be written on the kitchen calendar, in the diary and anywhere else where appointments are noted. These are fixtures like the Cup Final. They are unchangeable!

Everything today conspires against our having time alone together. Not only the pace of life, but even our children, whom we love, make it a lot harder for us to get time in peace on our own. We may believe or hope that living under the same roof will protect us against losing contact with each other, but it doesn't. It is even possible to share the same bed, yet drift into becoming strangers. As Margaret Mead says, 'There is no lonelier person than the one who lives with a spouse with whom he or she cannot communicate.'

Suppose for a minute that you've succeeded. You've made the time and you've found a place which is reasonably pleasant and free of interruption. Then what?

Begin by saying something nice!

'I'm so grateful that you made this time tonight.'

'How brilliant to have a bit of peace and quiet for a change!'

'This is a nice place!'

Enjoy the drink, relax, look at each other and smile! Then when you've both wound down a bit, start to find out from each other how the week has gone. How do you feel about it? And how does your partner feel about theirs? Work? Home? Children? Neighbours? Holiday plans, if any? The news? Cash flow? Aches and pains?

Then, having listened and shared these things, and talked through any problems and anxieties, we can begin to talk about ourselves, again starting with good moments, things we've appreciated or enjoyed about each other.

'The saucepan handle you mended is working fine.'

'That pie you made was delicious.'

'I like you in that colour blue. It really suits you.'

There will inevitably be misunderstandings and hurts as well.

Selective Hearing Syndrome - Female

As John drove home, he was looking forward to the treacle pudding that Jenny had suggested as a celebration of the weekend to come. But when the meal was put on the table, there was tinned fruit instead. Jenny tried to explain. 'I was too busy to do a pudding today in the end, and anyway, it's my "Keep fit" class tonight, so there wouldn't be time to dish it up. I'll have to be off in half an hour.' John was disappointed and a bit hurt too, but he just shrugged. With the children round the table, this wasn't the moment to say anything.

Even this sort of hurt needs to be shared at a suitable moment, gently, quietly, not accusingly, so that we can learn from what went wrong and work out a better way for next time. The absence of a treacle pudding isn't going to break a partnership, but lots of little disappointments and minor hurts add up to a big pile if they're left to accumulate. It's usually the small things that get to us – the straw that breaks the camel's back. When the children were in bed, and Jenny was back from her 'Keep fit' class, she and John sat down for a coffee.

John began, 'What made the day so hectic for you?'

'Oh, nothing special. The phone kept ringing, and I had that coffee morning to organise, and – well, to be honest, I forgot about the pudding till I was laying the table.'

'Never mind. We can have one another time. It was just such a delicious idea, that's all. I'd been looking forward to it all day, and when I couldn't smell hot treacle as I came in, I must admit to being rather disappointed.'

Jenny reached up and kissed him.

'Sorry, John. I'll make one for Sunday, I promise.'

John and Jenny didn't hide their feelings, and we mustn't either. Two minutes' conversation, and the molehill was flattened. No mountain was going to build here. They didn't hang up on each other, and nor should we. We simply can't afford to. We have to hang on – and let our partner say something.

DIY *Think of a time when your partner pleased you, and tell him or her as soon as you get the chance.*
Think of a time in the past when your partner looked bewildered or hurt. Use the next possible moment together to talk about it.

'Am I Getting Through?'

Sharing our feelings makes us vulnerable. It takes courage, because we are opening the door on an intimate part of our personality – our emotions. As we do this, we need to feel accepted by our partner, otherwise we shan't dare open up again. By sharing what we feel, we are letting our partner into the living room of our life. Our partner must take care not to trample about in muddy boots. A loving, accepting response is essential or we shall very rapidly dry up.

Paul (a teacher): 'I feel really depressed about school. The discipline seems to get worse and worse, and I sometimes wonder whether I'm actually teaching them anything.'
Diane: 'It's really getting you down, isn't it? I've noticed you've been a bit low recently. Do you think there's anything that could be done to help the situation?'
Paul: 'Well, maybe I could go and see the Head.'
Diane: 'Would he listen, d'you think?'
Paul: 'I don't know. He's not very good with his own children, I've noticed.'
Diane: 'What about a word with some of the parents?'
Paul: 'Yes, perhaps that would help. I might try that next week.'

To use the living-room picture, Diane trod delicately. She didn't trample about in muddy boots all over Paul's feelings. But she could have done.

Paul: 'I'm feeling really depressed about school. The discipline seems to get worse and worse, and I sometimes wonder whether I'm actually teaching them anything.'
Diane: 'Oh come off it, Paul. Of course you are! Children aren't that much worse than they used to be. Just shout a bit louder.'

This would have left Paul still depressed, and probably not daring to express his feelings about school again.

Is it a coincidence that we were given two ears and one mouth? Or does this mean that we should listen twice as much as we talk?

It's been said that 'some listen, some wait to speak'. Are we too eager to have our say, and quick to dismiss what our partner is trying to explain to us? Are we listeners, or those who merely wait to speak? How good is our hearing?

We need to teach our two ears a lesson – they must learn to hear, really hear, what is being said. And we need to teach our mouth a lesson too – to keep shut until the other has said it all.

How can we do this? There's no short-cut. We just have to practise till we get there. Every friendship is two-way. Would you go on seeing a friend if every time you met, the friend talked non stop, appeared totally uninterested in you and your life, and then jumped into their car and zoomed off? Yet that's how we can treat each other in our relationships sometimes.

Listen to the noise in your home. The TV's going, the children are squabbling over some sweets, the dog is whining for his dinner, the kettle's boiling, someone's

You have to be a whirling miracle!

on the phone, there's a knock at the door, the washing-machine is spinning, and so are you – trying to do five things at once while solving a maths homework problem and getting the five-year-old to do his reading. No wonder you can't hear – you can't hear yourself think, let alone listen to anyone else. You're a whirling miracle, accomplishing the job of cook, dad or mum, teacher, dog-owner, householder, husband or wife, peace-keeper – and all without burning or spilling anything, treading on the dog's tail or the two-year-old's latest masterpiece. This is not the setting for listening, is it?

We went through a stressful patch in our marriage a little while ago. In fact, it reached a point where we had to talk it through. My husband had a day of appointments, but he was able to cancel them all, and we spent the whole day together. The barriers came down. We managed to open up to each other. I shed many tears, and by the end we were together again. We'd listened to each other and understood, and had regained our normal closeness.

Pay each other the supreme compliment of stopping for a while, and really trying to listen to each other. Build your friendship by sharing the ups and downs of the day or the week. Iron out any misunderstandings before they get out of proportion. Forgetting to buy the apples wasn't an earth-shattering tragedy. Not passing on that message won't wreck your partner's career. Being half an hour late home isn't next to murder....

A quiet tone of voice, a few explanations and a bit of discussion can do wonders, like oil on a squeaky hinge or a warm iron on a crumpled skirt.

Remember, feelings are real and delicate. FRAGILE – HANDLE WITH CARE. We need to respect their reality, however illogical or foolish they may seem to us, and tread carefully.

DIY *Ask your partner: Do I listen to you? Do I understand how you're feeling?*
Next time your partner expresses a feeling, be like Diane. Accept it as real, and make it easy for your partner to share more.

Do's & Don'ts

- **Don't** expect a man to listen to you if he's hungry.
- **Do** find a time and a place that is comfortable and reasonably peaceful.
- **Do** give your full attention to your partner.
- **Don't** try to pour your heart out when your partner's dashing off to work.
- **Do** sit close to each other, and touch if you can.
- **Do** allow enough time.
- **Don't** let anything or anyone interrupt you unless absolutely necessary.
- **Do** your best to understand your partner's point of view.
- **Do** remember that men and women are very different!
- **Don't** lose your sense of humour!
- **Do** watch out for non-verbal signals – tone of voice, gesture, eyes.
- **Do it! Listen!**

PS Do choose a <u>creamy</u> custard pie if the urge to throw something becomes irresistible!

Spot the Blockages

Jim was made redundant one Friday afternoon without warning. He drove home in a daze, hardly believing the nightmare that had suddenly shattered his life.

As he walked through the door, Mary could see that something terrible had happened.

'What is it?' she asked quietly.

'I've been made redundant.'

'Redundant! But they can't just do that to you out of the blue!' said Mary angrily.

Jim hung his head. 'Well, they have,' he said.

'Oh Jim...how will we manage?'

Mary tried to choke back her tears as she saw the despair in Jim's face. She flung her arms round him.

'Whatever happens, you'll never be redundant to us,' she said defiantly. 'We'll always need you!'

Jim wrapped Mary in his arms. She couldn't have said anything better. It was tough, but whatever happened, he had his family.

Mary heard what Jim was saying and shared his shock and pain, so she was able to be a real comfort to him. We're not all like Mary. There are lots of blockages that stop us from hearing each other properly. Let's have a look at some of them.

It's so easy to go on the **defensive** as soon as a slightly critical remark is made:

David: 'I'm running out of shirts.'

Jill, crossly: 'How could I possibly get your b - shirts ironed this week, what with the kids down with chicken pox!'

David, voice rising: 'All right, all right! I'm not blaming you. I'm just saying that I don't have a shirt to wear in the morning.'

Jill, shouting: 'Well, go and iron your own b - shirts. I've just about had enough this week!'

The conversation could have gone differently:

David: 'I'm running out of shirts.'

Jill, quietly: 'I'm sorry, honey. I just haven't managed the ironing this week, what with the kids having chicken pox.'

David: 'That's OK, love. I'll iron some tonight. I think you need a rest!'

Instead of becoming defensive, backing off into a corner and starting to fight, at least verbally, how much better to admit where we didn't manage something or got it wrong. This way we give each other a chance to understand and be reasonable, to find ways to co-operate, and not to fight.

Pride can block our ears too. None of us likes to hear negatives about ourselves, so we block our ears and shout to drown the words that threaten us. But let's face it. None of us are angels – we all get it wrong sometimes. How much better to admit it than have a slanging match which leaves both of us hurt and bruised. Backing down takes a lot more courage than shouting back.

Self-centredness can also get in the way. When I'm primarily concerned with no. 1, I'm not likely to be interested in learning about my partner's feelings or difficulties – unless it affects no. 1.

Jan had a splitting headache when Brian came home, but he was too preoccupied to notice – until she was sick and had to abandon the cooking. That meant he'd have to do it, and be late for his game of darts. 'Blast it!' he muttered under his breath. 'Why tonight of all nights?'

His sympathy was more for himself than Jan. His self-centredness had blocked his ears to her need for loving care.

Tiredness is another old enemy. We all tend to get scratchy and operate on a short fuse when we're tired. The work load may be extra heavy, or one of the children is ill, we're not sleeping well, or Christmas is coming. I know that when mid-December comes, with

Hearing Selective Syndrome – Male

presents to buy, cakes to ice, mince pies to make, wrapping paper, ribbons, labels, candles, decorations and a thousand other things to remember, I tend to get very weary and difficult to communicate with. My husband Michael only has to say the wrong thing, or even the right thing at the wrong moment, and he will either get nothing back or I'll crumple up in a heap.

When this happens, he helps a lot by sitting down with me and gently asking me to tell him all the things that are bothering me or have to be done. Then we work out how to cope, or make short-cuts, or he takes over some things for me, and gradually the impossible mountain subsides to a manageable molehill.

It isn't always possible to avoid fatigue, but whenever we can get some rest and rise above the water-line again, it'll certainly help our relationships, at home and at work.

Excuse the question, but is anything blocking your ears? Has your personal Ansaphone made the long bleep, the signal for the caller to speak? Or is there a fault on the line, a blockage that needs to be removed?

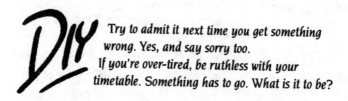

Try to admit it next time you get something wrong. Yes, and say sorry too.
If you're over-tired, be ruthless with your timetable. Something has to go. What is it to be?

'Slow Down, You Move Too Fast!'

A friend of mine has written a book, quite a slim paperback, called *Where Can I Find the Time?* She gave me a copy. 'The trouble is,' she said, as she handed it to me, 'I've given it to lots of friends, and they haven't had time to read it!'

If someone could invent a few more hours in the day, and sell them at £1 or even £10 each, I'm sure they'd be a billionaire in next to no time. We all want more time – time to spend with our children, a few minutes to catch up, the chance for more exercise, an extra hour of sleep, time to play, the opportunity for longer holidays, time for more work, moments to be alone, time with our marriage partner, leisure to weed the garden, take the dog for a walk, wash the car, write letters, pay the bills, do the shopping, visit a neighbour, have friends in, read, make Amanda's birthday cake, and time to STOP.

We run and rush and dash and hurry. We have gadgets that help us cook faster, clean faster, do the washing faster, print and photo-copy faster, yet we still find ourselves on the run.

'I've got five minutes before I need to leave. I'll just make a phone call/peel the potatoes/look at the post....' It's so easy to think like this, and the result is that we leave late and drive under pressure, adding a further stress factor to the day as we sit behind a slow bus or tractor and watch the minutes tick by.

'Never walk if you can run,' seems to be my motto, and 'never walk peacefully if you can walk urgently.' 'Don't relax in a chair. Sit on the edge. You may need to leap up in two minutes.' 'Have a chat in the doorway. Don't come in and sit down. There's a job to be done any minute.'

Despite all this apparent pressure, the undone things pile up – an old lady who needs a visit; some files that were going to be tidied when the last child started at day-school – twelve years ago!; shelves still not put up; the car accumulating dirt and longing for a polish.

The humbling fact is that we all have exactly the same amount of time, even the Prime Minister – twenty-four hours a day. There isn't a human being on this earth who has one minute more or one minute less. So what's the matter with us? Why are we living as if the world's going to stop tomorrow, and everything must be crammed into these last few hours?

Perhaps the world **will** stop tomorrow. Will we be glad then, with the way we've used the time we had? It's a sobering thought.

A West Highlander was once sitting on a mountainside with a friend from the South of England.

'Tell me,' said the Highlander. 'Is it true that in the South, the pace of life is much faster than here?'

'Yes, I'm afraid it is,' replied his friend. 'It seems as if everyone's always in a hurry down there.'

There was a long pause, then the Highlander said thoughtfully, almost to himself, 'Who wants to hurry?'

Who indeed? Yet most of us do it, most of the time. We seem to have an internal need to hurry. Perhaps it's because we need to be seen to be important, to feel valuable, even invaluable.

Gavin and Annie were on the run as usual. By the time the last child was in bed, they crashed onto the settee exhausted.

'What's the matter with us?' said Annie. 'It's always the same. By this time of day, you can count me out. I'm finished. And you're exhausted too. Must it go on like this for ever? Why is every day like a marathon? If someone had told me that running a home and bringing up three young children was this hectic, I might have thought twice.'

Gavin was quiet for a minute, then he took Annie's hand in his.

'Let's think it through,' he said. 'I don't think it has to be this way, and certainly not if it makes you unhappy and constantly weary.' They discussed the things that had to be done, and the things Annie liked doing such as going to the Mums and Toddlers group, and then looked at all the other items on her daily and weekly agenda. With Gavin's help, Annie put a line through several evening meetings, school commitments and a few other things, and sat down then and there to write letters of explanation and resignation to the various people concerned.

Gavin had a look at his diary too. It was chock-a-block with engagements for several weeks ahead. They read it together, and began to see things that he could drop when the next AGM came up, or he could probably find someone without small children to take over for him.

They agreed some reasonable limits to the amount of time they each spent on evening commitments, sport and leisure, church and other local meetings. They also decided that certain things came into the category of 'non-negotiable time'. For example, family Sunday dinner, children's bed-time, one evening a week alone together – **not** for doing chores but for being and talking. They put family birthdays, an annual anniversary dinner and promised outings into this category too.

By the time they had both finished, they felt quite excited.

'In a few months' time, we'll be wondering what to do!' Annie laughed.

'In a few months' time, we may be getting to know each other again!' said Gavin, and gave Annie a squeeze.

Some of us have become more like time machines than people, with our watches and Filofaxes, appointments and schedules. 'I can't stop. I'll miss the train.' 'I can't come and see you this week. The diary's full.' Time seems to drive us. It has become more important than people. It dictates our lives more than our feelings or even our conscience sometimes. It rules us – but should it? Is life in some way better when time rules? I don't really believe it is, and I suspect that you don't either. So how do we escape, get out of the rut? 'Stop the world – I want to get off!' – even if it's only for five minutes.

What's pressurising us into doing all those things, trying to fulfil all those responsibilities? Where has the desperate 'but I've *got to*' feeling come from?

Is it that everyone else is running, so we feel we must keep up? When I look around at some of my friends and see what they get through in a week, it makes me wonder what I do with myself – yet I don't seem to sit down very much. There's a hidden pressure – 'They do it, so I ought to be able to manage it too.' Anybody would think we were born to be human doings, not human beings. There's so little time just to be.

Is it that we can't say, 'No,' when we're asked to help with this, join that or give time to the other? We need to develop 'won't-power' as well as will-power. The power and the courage to say, 'No, sorry, I won't.'

Let's face it. What if the boss is less pleased, the committee loses a member, the car isn't clean, the club sees less of you than it used to? The choices we've made may still be better for ourselves and our family.

What do you do if you see a fifteen or thirty-minute space in the day – if such a phenomenon ever occurs in your life? How do you use your 'lunch hour' at work? Do you fill these times with doing things? I know I do. But how about developing a new system? Why not use that time to relax, read a book or magazine, take some

time out of life's busyness. Impossible? Why? You might be much nicer for the rest of the day if you'd treated yourself to that little oasis of peace.

The diary could even become an ally. A very busy 'at-home' mother who was constantly on the edge of tears from exhaustion, started to put half-hour or even sometimes hour-long 'engagements' in her diary. She thought of a name for them – a good one might be your own second name if you have one, or you could use your initials, or 'Stop!' or anything which says to you that this is your time. Seeing it in the diary makes it easier to use it for yourself when the time comes, as well as preventing it from getting booked up with anyone or anything else.

For working parents, the hurry disease has bitten them hard. It can feel as if a whirlwind has hit the house when they get home. Yet the hopeful voice of a little boy, 'Dad, will you play football with me?' or the little girl who says hopefully, 'Mum, do you like my painting?' or, 'Do you know what happened at school today?' is barely heard. 'Sorry, son, no time today.' 'Lovely painting, darling.' The children can tell that their Mum and Dad aren't really listening.

Can't it wait?

Who or what is more important than the wife you fell in love with and said you wanted to share your life with? Who or what takes priority over two precious children who look to you as their one and only Dad and Mum, and are quietly, yet with all their hearts, needing your attention and approval? Can't it wait for just ten minutes, even thirty minutes, while these young VIPs in your life get your full attention? To a child, ten or thirty minutes is a long time. Given on a regular basis, this amount of attention could build a close and deeply rewarding relationship. Will the world fall apart if you make it wait that long?

Put it this way. What may appear to you to be a fairly short time with your children is worth to them ten, twenty, thirty times as much as the same amount of

34

minutes invested in your work or social affairs. Fathers and mothers who spend time with their children when the children are young are likely to reap a rich reward of friendship and pleasure in their relationship with them in later life.

Again, undivided attention between husband and wife is of more value in the long term than winning the pools. If it happens daily, or even weekly, the likelihood of a healthy, happy marriage is going to increase dramatically. It would be difficult to exaggerate the importance of spending time together.

People matter most of all. If we're trampling over people and spending all our time on work and activity, however worthy, everyone is going to be the loser in the end, including ourselves.

There's a prayer that starts:

Lord, I have time,
I have plenty of time,
All the time that you give me,
The years of my life,
The days of my years,
The hours of my days,
They are all mine....

It's what we do with the time we have that matters.

DIY Write some STOP *gaps into your diary. Make time together to take a careful look at your schedules. Ensure that your top priorities come out top.*

'Happily Ever After...'

It had been a wonderful wedding – glorious sunshine, a beautiful service, radiant bride and bridegroom, happy guests, good photographs – and then away to a week's honeymoon in a romantic guest house on the edge of Exmoor.

Mark and Brenda had known each other for ten months before they married. They met when Brenda came to Mark's workplace to do some market research, and since then, they'd done almost everything together. Now they were married, and busy trying to get their one-bedroomed flat organised.

Brenda didn't like the vinyl flooring; she wanted carpets, but Mark said they couldn't afford it.

'Well, I'll pay for it out of my wages,' said Brenda.

'We've got a joint bank account now, remember? And don't forget the mortgage, and the payments for the car.'

'But it's so cold and noisy without carpets, and it takes so much longer to clean.'

The argument went to and fro till Brenda burst into tears.

'We only got back from our honeymoon yesterday, and we're quarrelling already.'

Mark put an arm round her shoulder and lent her a hanky.

'Come on, let's go out for a pizza. We can sort it out later.'

'The prince met the princess and they fell in love....

Then they married and lived happily ever after.' So say the fairy tales, but marriage isn't a fairy tale. It's about real people with real personalities, people with likes and dislikes, faults and weaknesses, varying expectations and different priorities.

Mark and Brenda found the first few weeks in their new flat tough. Mark came from a happy-go-lucky, untidy home with a warm, friendly family who laughed a lot and didn't use the duster or vacuum cleaner very often.

Brenda's mother was house proud and liked the place to be 'just so'. Her father earned a good wage, but didn't say much when he was at home. He watched the telly or tinkered with the car.

Mark felt trapped in the little flat with a rather quiet wife, and often suggested they go home (to his parents) for a meal. He longed for a good laugh and the warmth of his family. Brenda felt trapped too. She hated the tattiness of the place, and felt angry with Mark for not allowing her to buy carpets and a decent suite for the living room.

Their dreams of marriage began to fade, till an older friend came by one day. They sat down for a cuppa.

'How are you two doing?' he asked. 'Thrown any good plates lately?!' They laughed, but were both secretly relieved that Andrew didn't expect everything to be perfect bliss.

'When we got married...' he began, and went on to share with them some of the disasters and traumas of the early days.

'We had some bad moments in the kitchen. I put one of our best dishes with gold trimming into the microwave and wrecked it. Then Anne made a delicious-looking chocolate cake, only she used salt instead of sugar!

'I completely forgot her birthday too. She sulked about

that for days – till I bought her a *huge* bouquet of flowers and took her out to dinner.

'She asked me one day when I was going to put the rubbish out. "That's your job, not mine," I said. "No, it's yours!" she insisted, and it turned out that her Dad always did it at home, whereas in my family, it was Mum's chore. When the bin was overflowing, we had to sort out who was going to do it. We decided that I'd do the rubbish bin and she'd do the ironing.

'We squabbled over where to put the ornaments, how to fit up the kitchen, whether to have a mobile phone, which supermarket was cheaper, who could use the car on Saturdays and when.

'Every time she put on new clothes I asked her how much they'd cost, when she wanted me to say how nice she looked.'

Mark and Brenda sat listening, and the more Andrew talked, the more they laughed. It was the laughter of huge relief. So they weren't odd after all! Other couples had struggled too.

'What's it like now?' Mark asked.

'Oh, it's miles better now,' said Andrew. 'We've sorted out lots of things, and on the whole we get along fine.'

'How did you do it?' said Brenda. 'What's the secret?'

Mark thought for a moment. 'I suppose there were several things,' he said. 'First of all, we decided after one particularly nasty quarrel, that we were going to make it. "We're not going to give up," we said to each other. "We're going to work at it."

'Anne wrote out the words from the wedding service, twice over. "All that I am I give to you, and all that I have I share with you." She stuck one copy over the bathroom mirror and another on the fridge! That helped us.

'Then I read a magazine one day. It said that marriage was a skill to be learned, like any other skill. It really struck me. I took years to learn engineering skills and get good at my job. Anne trained for years before she set up as a physio., so why should we suddenly be good at being married, when we were only at the very beginning?

'We've got our L-plates on,' we said to each other. 'No wonder we make lots of mistakes, but we're certainly not giving up. Practice makes perfect and we're getting plenty of practice! Who knows? Perhaps we'll have a perfect marriage one day!'

Mark and Brenda looked at each other. 'I'm going to put an L-plate on the wall,' said Brenda, 'then every time we start quarrelling, we can say to each other, "We're only learners!" and try again.'

Andrew smiled. 'Good luck!' he said. 'You'll make it.' Then he left. But for Mark and Brenda, a new chapter had begun. They were learners. They put the L-plate on the wall and stuck a copy of their marriage promises on the bedroom cupboard. They still crossed each other quite a bit, but they had a new determination.

'We're going to learn. We're going to get good at this business, this new skill called marriage.'

They decided that when they'd had a tough patch, they'd go out for the evening and have fun. It helped to relieve the tension and make them feel good again.

When they managed to agree about something without getting angry or upset, they sometimes celebrated by buying a box of chocolates or having a glass of wine. And gradually they began to sort out their differences and enjoy each other more and more.

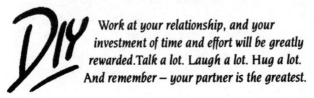 Work at your relationship, and your investment of time and effort will be greatly rewarded. Talk a lot. Laugh a lot. Hug a lot. And remember – your partner is the greatest.

Forgive and Forget

Isolated lily leaves on the surface of a pond, touching only when the wind blows, yet joined by the stalk at the root. Balloons held in the air, separated as each child takes a string, touching only when the children come close together. Magnets, drawn to each other, yet thrust apart when reversed.

What keeps us together and what keeps us apart?

Look at yesterday. Did I give a sharp answer when I needn't have done, and then not apologise? Did I turn away crossly when my husband said he was sorry not to have rung to say he'd be late – and then sulk all evening? Was I angry with my wife for using bleach on my shirt and ruining it – even though she said she'd get me a new one? Did we quarrel about whose turn it was to get up to look after the baby in the night, or pay for the TV licence, or wash the windows – and hang on to our anger?

Like the lily leaves or the balloons, touching in the wind but held apart, we can live in an isolation created by unforgiveness.

'I'm sorry I was so cross when you asked about the plumber coming. It's just that I'd rung him three times, and then the day sort of took over, and when you got in, I was ready to drop.'

'That's OK, love. Not to worry. I'll ring him myself in the morning.'

'You should at least have rung and told me you were delayed. I was worried sick, and the children wouldn't settle because you hadn't said goodnight.'

'I'm so sorry. I didn't realise just how late I was going to be. I really am sorry to have worried you so.'

'All right. I forgive you, but please ring another time. We do hate it when you don't come home.'

'How could you wreck my shirt by putting bleach on it? *Bleach,* I ask you? That's guaranteed to ruin it!'

'I just couldn't get that stain out, so I thought a bit of bleach might do the trick.'

'Well, it didn't, did it? Look at it now! Great yellow stains on the front! Absolutely unwearable! What a waste of money. I've only had it a month.'

'I'm *terribly* sorry. I made a real mess of it. I'll save up and buy you another one if you like, or I could try dyeing it a darker colour?'

'I don't *want* a darker colour! I wanted the ivory one. That's why I got it.'

'Oh dear. I'm so, so sorry. Please forgive me. Please don't let's let a shirt ruin our whole weekend.'

'It was exactly the shirt I've been looking for for ages, and they didn't have another ivory one in my size.'

He stomped out of the kitchen and banged the door. She sat on a stool and cried. Like balloons pulled apart by children, his unforgiveness had pulled them apart, and it hurt.

Sometimes it's the tiny things that draw us together or push us away from each other.

'You didn't kiss me goodnight last night.'

'Didn't I? I must have fallen asleep. Here's two big ones to make up for it!'

'You're very quiet,' she said.

He shrugged, with a hurt look.

'Have I done something?'

'I wish you wouldn't correct me in the middle when I'm telling a story. You kept doing it at supper last night.'

'I'm *so* sorry. I'm afraid I just blurt it out before I can stop myself. But I *must* learn not to. Please forgive me.'

He turned to her. Their eyes met and love was there. He kissed her, and it was all right again.

'Marriage is starting to love, over and over again.'

Robert Quillen said, 'A happy marriage is the union of two good forgivers.'

Every time we say sorry, every time we forgive, we start loving again. We come closer.

Every time we stay cross, refuse to forgive, or hang on to our resentment, a tiny fragment of our love dies. We draw further apart.

Tony and Caroline had been married for ten years, and although they'd started off fairly happily, things had become very difficult. Three small children, a shortage of money, and long working hours had all taken their toll, and they now found it hard to be pleasant to each other at all. They shouted and quarrelled about almost everything, hurting each other with cutting words. Yet deep down, they still loved each other, and they could see how unhappy they were making the children as well as themselves. They went to friends they could trust for help.

Their friends listened while they both explained what was happening, and then asked them whether they were serious about wanting to put the past behind them and make a go of their marriage.

'Yes,' they said. 'We are.'

Their friends encouraged them to share in turn,

calmly, all the ways in which the other had hurt or upset them. All this 'rubbish' was then thrown into an imaginary dustbin, and they expressed real forgiveness to each other.

Once they had done this, they held hands and repeated their marriage vows to each other. 'To have and to hold, from this day forward, for better, for worse, for richer, for poorer, in sickness and in health, till death us do part.... I give you my solemn vow.'

Their marriage was reborn that day. The following months weren't easy. Old habits die hard. They needed further help and encouragement from their friends. But every time an old resentment surfaced, an old habit tried to reassert itself, they determined to stop it, and made the decision to love, to forgive and to go on.

Sometimes it's not a day-to-day matter, but something much bigger.

Chris and Susie were not on speaking terms. Susie was expecting their first baby, but during this time Chris was having an affair. Susie was miserable and angry, and finally told Chris to get out.

He went, but soon he found that the new 'friends' he was mixing with had disappeared. They didn't want to know. Nor did the girlfriend.

Then the baby was due, his baby, and he decided he must be there. Susie was still hurt and angry, but she let him come to the hospital where she gave birth to a beautiful little boy. Both of them were thrilled and when Susie came out of hospital, Chris moved back into the flat, but she wouldn't let him near her. She wanted to punish him for being so cruel to her.

After a while, Chris couldn't stand it any more. He knew he had to do something. One evening after supper when they were having coffee, he began: 'Susie, I'm desperately sorry for the way I've hurt you.'

At first Susie turned away, but as Chris went on and reached out to take her hand, she turned towards him with tears in her eyes. She poured out the pain and hurt of the past weeks, her loneliness without him, her fear of being on her own with the baby, her anger and her sense of shame and failure.

Chris listened and held her hand. When she'd finished, he gently lifted her up and wrapped his arms round her, while she sobbed and sobbed into his sweater.

'I'm sorry, I'm sorry,' he kept saying quietly, and at long last the tears subsided. 'I'd no idea how much I'd hurt you. Will you ever be able to forgive me? Can we ever be really together again?'

Susie held him tight. 'I do forgive you,' she said, 'but it'll be hard to trust you now – I'll need time. But I do still love you, Chris, and I want us to be together.'

They hugged again – a long, warm hug. Susie blew her nose, and they were ready to try again.

It has been said: 'To sin is human, to forgive, divine.'

Forgiveness is not a feeling. It is a decision that we make. It is not true to say, 'I can't forgive.' The truth is either, 'I won't,' or, 'I haven't yet learned how to.' If we are willing, we will be able to do it in the end. If the hurt is deep, though, it will take time. A decision may need to be made again and again, when bitterness or anger come knocking on our door.

One husband said to another, 'Sometimes my wife becomes quite historical.'

'Don't you mean hysterical?'

'No, no, historical. She brings up all the things I've ever done wrong.'

No doubt these 'historical' conversations were full of statements beginning: 'You always...', 'You never...', showing clearly that the injured wife hadn't forgiven her husband at all. She'd kept a drawer full of his misdeeds which she used as verbal missiles whenever she was angry.

We need to forgive and, as far as possible, forget, which involves a conscious decision not to bring that thing up again.

Did you ever get a bad report from school? Or a less-than-good reference from an employer? When we are forgiven, it's as if that report or reference was torn to shreds. It no longer exists and cannot be used against us. That's forgiveness – to tear to shreds the hurts that others have done to us, and never attempt to piece them together again.

Rob and Karen appeared to have a good marriage, but Rob had an affair that lasted several months. Karen never found out, but in the end, Rob couldn't live with the lie. His sense of guilt was making him utterly miserable, and had built a powerful, silent barrier between him and Karen. Yet Karen would be shattered. How could he ever tell her? And would she ever forgive him?

He sought advice from his church minister who warned him: 'That one lie will prove deeply corrosive.' The minister encouraged him to tell Karen, despite the terrible hurt it would cause, because unless he did, their marriage could never thrive again. The lie would eat away at their love and destroy it.

Karen was utterly shocked. She couldn't believe it to start with. Then she began asking questions endlessly: 'How did it start? Where did you meet? How often?'

For nights and nights they lay awake, while Karen sobbed and Rob did his best to comfort her.

'How sorry was he?' she wanted to know. 'How could she be sure he wouldn't do it again? Would he ever again want to make love to her, and did she want him to?'

Slowly, as the weeks went painfully by, they worked their way through, with the support of their minister and his wife, until finally Karen was able to say from her heart, 'I forgive you, Rob,' and Rob was able, at last, to accept her forgiveness and forgive himself for the terrible hurt he'd caused.

Rob and Karen are now more in love than they've ever been before. Forgiveness brought healing, healing restored love, and love rekindled romance. The way back wasn't easy, but it was worth every step.

DIY Are you angry, resentful or bitter about something? Discuss it if you can, and decide to forgive.

Are you guilty of hurting your partner? Confess it, express real sorrow and ask for forgiveness.

Are you keeping something secret from your partner which is causing a rift in your marriage?

If you need help in these areas, don't hesitate to seek it. It's all too easy to confess something in order to get rid of your own guilt, but not to have the will to be forgiven and to make a new start. Do you want to forgive your partner? And be forgiven?

Be Big – Back Down!

o you believe in fairy stories? 'The Prince married the Princess and took her to a beautiful castle where they lived happily ever after....' How come they were so happy so easily? Was it that they had lots of servants and lots of money, so they could click their fingers and do exactly what they liked whenever they fancied? Well, that would certainly help.

Or was it that the castle was huge, and each of them had their own apartments so that they only met for banquets and celebrations and romantic nights in the royal suite? In that case there would be little cause for conflict, but there probably wasn't much intimacy either, because their time together would be too special and rare for them to grow close and share their hearts with each other.

Anyway, we are living in the real world. No fairy stories for us. Quite possibly we have very limited space and money, and little support from our wider family, who may live far away, or from the community in which we live. And, let's face it, we all have our faults and will sometimes be selfish or obstinate or proud. Each of these factors can cause problems and arguments.

In addition to this, the expectations we have of marriage are so high that they could probably never be fulfilled, and the disappointment this brings can make for problems too. We may have expected each day to be gloriously sunny and smiling: each night to be wonderfully romantic and satisfying: each evening to be spent sitting closely together watching telly, talking, listening to our latest CD; every weekend to include lovely outings together; in fact, our whole life pattern to be perfect bliss....

women have spread themselves too thin with this juggling of marriage, career, and children

right as usual dear, marriage will have to go

Whoever gave us that idea? By what magic can two totally individual people, suddenly sharing every detail of their lives together, fuse into a beautiful, harmonious oneness overnight? Mary Hathaway, in her book *Celebrating Marriage*, says, 'I learned that love has to grow. You don't plant an acorn today and expect to see an oak tree tomorrow.' Whoever suggested that such a skill could be learned without effort and trials along the way? If it takes four years to qualify as a teacher, seven years to become an architect and many years to become an expert cook, how could we possibly think for one second that the skills, unselfishness, self-control, thoughtfulness and genuine communication that go to make a happy marriage could be learned in less time than these other professions?

Are you a thoughtful, unselfish person? And what about your partner? A happy life living together can only be happy if two kind, considerate people are in it together. All our faults and failings are magnified at close quarters, so unless we deal with them in ourselves, our dream is still a long way off.

It's a great mistake to think we can change someone after marriage. We can do our best to change ourselves, we can try to alter our own attitudes, but not theirs. So if we'd rather live peaceably and be able to resolve our differences without having a row, how do we go about it? Here are some hints for harmony.

1. Keep your voice down. There's a proverb which says, 'A soft answer turns away wrath, but a harsh one stirs it up.' It's true. Try it.

2. Avoid sweeping accusations like 'You always...' and 'You never....' They're usually untrue anyway. Remember, the more mud you sling, the more ground you lose.

3. Use non-confrontational phrases like 'I wonder whether...', 'What do you feel...?', 'Have you thought about....'

4. Try to work out why certain things make one of you angry – and talk it through together when the storm is over.

5. If there is a recurrent problem, take time to work out a solution together.

Jeremy and Ruth had in-law problems. Jeremy's parents insisted that they go to them every Christmas, and always turn up for family birthdays and anniversaries, but none of the family liked going. Grandad was deaf and sat reading most of the time, and Grandmum was often flustered and cross.

Ruth's Dad had died, and her Mum lived alone. She only had a small cottage, so it was quite a squash, but she was always warm and welcoming, baking chocolate cakes for the children, playing games after tea, and putting special little things out for them to look at and play with. Everyone loved going to Nan's.

Jeremy's mum rang up one day, assuming that the family were coming for Christmas, and this time Jeremy didn't give in.

'We're not sure about our plans yet, Mum. I'll let you know in a few days.'

His mother was furious.

'What do you mean, "You'll let me know"? Of course you're coming.'

'I'm just not sure yet, Mum. It's very kind of you to ask us, but we've got a few things to work out. May I ring you soon? Forgive me. I must dash to a meeting now. 'Bye.'

He left his mother speechless with rage and shock on the other end of the line. He and Ruth discussed the problem. What would be fair? How could they go to Nan's without hurting Grandmum and Grandad too much? They decided that Jeremy should write a letter. In it, he'd explain that he still loved his parents, but reminding them that he was now thirty-five, had been married for ten years, had a demanding job, and was a husband and father with many responsibilities. He was no longer a little boy to be ordered about. He needed to be free to make his own decisions.

'Can't we be good friends now?' he concluded. 'We can invite you and you can invite us, and we can have a grown-up friendship. It'd be so good. We want to see you, but please understand that we'd rather not just be taken for granted.'

His parents were very upset when they first read

Listen carefully to what your partner is saying!

Jeremy's letter, but as they thought about it, they began to realise that they had been treating him as if he were still their little boy. They eventually wrote back apologising, and agreeing that it'd be good to be friends. The family spent half of Christmas with them and half with Ruth's Mum, and the problem began to get sorted out.

A few more hints

6. If it's a **sit-down-and-talk affair**, eat first!

7. Don't try to discuss problems if you're over-tired. But do tackle the tiredness or you'll never tackle the problems.

8. Sit next to each other rather than opposite. Your common enemy is the conflict, not each other. Alternatively, go for a walk or a drive while you talk it over. It's often easier to discuss sensitive things when you're doing something active, and it's more relaxed.

9. Don't bring up past arguments and failings. Let bygones be bygones.

10. Listen carefully, and show that you've heard by saying what you think your partner is feeling or trying to explain. For example, a wife might say, 'When people come to a meal, you stay with them and talk, while I do all the clearing. I find that really hard. It makes me feel resentful and angry.'

'You feel angry and find it hard that I don't come and help. I'm so sorry, I never realised. How else can we work it out?'

11. Keep your **sense of humour**.

12. Don't walk away, even if you cry. Unresolved conflicts don't go away, they hang around and build up. Feelings that are buried are buried alive, and they will rise again.

13. Don't go to sleep without sorting it out. 'Quit the flak before you hit the sack.'

14. Backing down works wonders. No one is always right. But it needs to be both who back down at times, not always the same partner. It takes more courage to back down than to defend the position. Be big. Back down!

15. Concentrate on your **own need to change**, not your partner's.

16. Say sorry – and forgive. It's the only way to let go of old hurts and pain. We have to learn to apologise and to give forgiveness.

It can be very tempting to 'punish' our partner when we feel they've let us down. We may refuse to talk or touch or kiss, not look at the other, refuse sex, or withdraw from household tasks. There are many ways of being subtly or not so subtly unkind to each other, and we may feel justified in doing this – but it isn't going to build our marriage! It simply drives us further apart as we nurse our grievance against our partner. It helps to look beyond the present and see how much we really love each other and value our relationship. Happiness lies in making up and moving on.

It isn't always easy...

Remember that a resolved conflict is quickly forgotten, but one that is unresolved is stored up and remembered, causing increasing bitterness and anger. Then one day we blow up in fury over some tiny thing like a dirty finger-mark on the cupboard or a door accidentally banged. A powder-keg, once well filled, takes only a very small spark to make it explode. Let's do our best to keep it empty by sorting things out as they arise.

Let's learn to be big – and back down!

Think of something you have not yet sorted out with your partner make time in the next day or two to set things right – perhaps over a cup of coffee.

'I Want' Gets Nothing

*C*ome with me on a walk down Any Street in Anytown, and let's peep through the windows.

At no. 41, Robert is lounging in front of the telly, while Sue dashes around trying to lay the table, cook the sausages, put the youngest to bed and stop the boys from fighting.

'Shut up, you two!' shouts Robert to the boys, and goes on watching telly.

At no. 52, the young couple have both just got in from work. Jen is putting some washing in the machine, while Hal is burrowing in the freezer for a possible microwave supper. They take the dog for a quick walk in the park, chatting about their different days, hot up the meal when they get home, and have it together.

At no. 60, a middle-aged couple are shouting at each other.

'You've been on that telephone for half an hour, and I've got some business calls coming through!'

'Well, I needed to make arrangements for tomorrow's meeting.'

'You women are always arranging meetings. I must get these calls or we may lose the deal.'

'Well, whose telephone is it anyway? I didn't think it was your personal possession.'

At no. 83, another argument is going on, while the

three small children watch anxiously.

'A golf tournament? On Saturday? But you can't! It's Emily's birthday party and she desperately wants you to be there – and the boys will run riot without you. Besides, have you forgotten that I'm in the Amateur Dramatics' production in the evening?'

'Well, I'm sorry, but the tournament's been fixed for ages, and I can't get out of it now.'

'Emily's birthday's been fixed for seven years, and I told you about the production back in January.'

At no. 87, Mum is preparing tea. She's had a dreadful day at work, and now she has a splitting headache, but two noisy children are clamouring for food. Her husband arrives home, with the weekly supermarket shopping, gives her a kiss, and sees at once that she's close to tears. He kisses her again and whispers, 'You go and lie down. I'll see to the children.' Thankfully, oh so thankfully, she climbs the stairs and curls up under the duvet, exhausted.

At no. 92, the husband is unemployed, so he's looking after the children and his wife is working as a nurse. Money is short, but it's Mum's birthday, so they've planned a little surprise. They've iced some biscuits in very bright colours, made some rather sickly fudge, and done a big birthday card saying 'HAPY BURFDAY MUM'.

A day at the hospital is always exhausting, but Mum hugs them all warmly and is really touched by the trouble they've taken. They have a happy-birthday tea and Mum admires the biscuits and says the fudge is delicious!

It doesn't take us long to spot the selfish and unselfish people behind these front doors, and to see where selfishness leads. We all want it our way, at least sometimes, but how about a bit of compromise?

Would it have been possible to arrange Emily's party for another day, then go to the Amateur Dramatics after the Golf Tournament, and enjoy the party without any time pressure? A discussion about the use of the telephone might have led to a solution such as taking it in turns, or using it for fifteen minutes each.

'I', 'me', 'my', 'mine', 'I want', 'I'm going to…' usually indicate a selfish attitude.

'You', 'we', 'our', 'What shall we do?', 'How are you this evening?' usually indicate an unselfish, thoughtful attitude.

Fred had a great love of old cars, and enjoyed nothing more than going to vintage car rallies. Helen understood that, and they worked out a plan whereby he went off to rallies sometimes, and at other times he looked after the children while she went off to meet a friend and go shopping. That way, everyone was happy.

Graham and Marie had to work things out too.

Marie liked buying clothes. She tended to get her pay cheque and go shopping on the way home, bringing back yet another skirt or pair of jeans or scarf. The trouble was, Graham knew they couldn't afford it.

'But you buy steaks and wine sometimes. What's the difference? At least my clothes are still there in the morning.'

'Good point, but clothes cost a lot more than food.'

'Good point.'

They talked about it and agreed on spending limits for both of them. It was tough at first, specially for Marie, but it worked.

Selfishness – 'I want it my way' – is like wiping your dirty shoes all over your partner, treating them as a door-mat, beneath your feet and beneath your consideration. It says, 'I count for more than you. I come first. What I want and what I like comes top of the list.' Unselfishness values others by putting them first, considering their views, being prepared to give in to their desires. It's an essential ingredient for happiness in marriage.

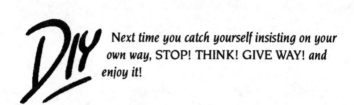 Next time you catch yourself insisting on your own way, STOP! THINK! GIVE WAY! *and enjoy it!*

Mind Your Ps and Qs

'Say please!' We train our children repeatedly over several years until the message finally gets home. 'Thank Mrs Jackson for having you.' 'Don't forget to shake hands when you meet Mr Thomas.' 'Have you written to Aunt Janet to thank her for your birthday present?' 'Don't just rush on when you've bumped into me. Say, "Excuse me," or, "Sorry, Mum."'

Then with our teenagers, it's more likely to be: 'Please tell me where you're going and when you'll be back.' 'Will you need a meal tonight?' 'Are you bringing friends home?' 'Could you let me know your plans for next weekend? I'm shopping today.'

But what happens between us as a couple?

When guests come, we tend to be extra attentive and thoughtful.

'Let me put your coat here.'

'Do sit by the fire where it's warm.'

'Would you like a drink?'

If they bring a small gift, we are generous with our thanks, and at the meal we try to pass them whatever they need and make sure they are well looked after.

In the early days of a new friendship, the same things may be true. The man may open the passenger door for his girlfriend to get into the car, compliment her on her appearance, carry her parcels and show her attention in lots of little ways.

She, enjoying his kindness, may respond warmly and happily to this feeling of being treated as someone special, thanking him for his kindnesses and saying how much she appreciates him.

What happens to all this attentiveness and good manners after a year or two of marriage? Where do those years of childhood training disappear?

Simon has just got in from work.

'Hello, love,' he calls. 'Just going to get my overalls off,' and he pounds upstairs. Five minutes later he comes to the kitchen.

'Kettle boiling? I could do with a cuppa.'

No greeting. No kiss. No 'How's the day been?' from either of them. Viv makes the tea and bangs it down on the table. Without even a 'thank you', Simon picks up the tray and makes for the door. Then over his shoulder he says, 'By the way, Viv, I've asked Barry and Jon round. I hope that's OK? We've got a lot of business to discuss.'

'Well, I'll have to manage, won't I?' Viv bites her lip as Simon heads for the telephone.

'Thanks, love. I knew you would,' and he's gone.

Roger and Gina are rather different. It was Saturday morning, and they'd decided to clear out the conservatory. Roger insisted on doing all the heavy lifting.

'I don't want you carting these chairs around,' he said. 'Why don't you get the broom and a bucket of water so we can wash the place down a bit.'

'Fine. Thanks very much.'

After about an hour's work, Gina suggests a cup of coffee.

'Brilliant idea. Yes, please! And let's have a biscuit too. We've earned it.'

Gina jerks the tray as she puts it down.

'Oh dear, I've spilt the coffee. I'm sorry. I'll get a cloth.'

'No, no, I'll get it.'

Do we still say 'thank you' every time our partner brings us something, passes the jam at table, mends a fuse, does a vase of flowers, irons a pile of shirts or fetches the car on a wet night?

Do we still say 'please' when we'd like him or her to do something for us? Phrases like: 'Do you think you could...?' or 'When you have time, I'd be so grateful if...' or 'Would it be possible to...?' show that we are aware of our partner, of their time pressure and busyness, and that we're not taking them, their time or their help for granted.

Do we apologise quickly whenever there is the slightest need – whether it's spilt coffee, a forgotten phone message or too sharp an answer in a moment of irritation? Even if it's not strictly our fault, we surely regret the mess, inconvenience or damage we've caused, and an immediate: 'I'm terribly sorry' or 'Oh dear, I do apologise' makes it much easier to pick up the pieces and move on.

If we've been grumpy or bad-tempered during the day, it really helps if we can say how sorry we are and ask forgiveness. I often need to do this when busyness, preoccupation or tiredness have made me irritable or unresponsive. Then we talk it over, and that helps too.

Do we still make a point of greeting each other when one has been out, even if only for a few hours?

Michael and I are in and out of the house a lot. He farms and has his office at home, and I seem to go out quite a bit. This gives us lots of opportunities to greet each other, which we much enjoy. There's always a 'coo-ee' when one of us gets home, and we have a kiss and often a hug. It's good to be together again.

Greetings can be so warm. If you come in from work or a meeting, and your partner gets up or stops what they're doing, comes to you with a smile, and gives you a warm kiss and a hug, doesn't that make you feel good?

On the other hand, if the one who comes home immediately plunges into a new activity with hardly a 'hello', or the one who was at home just carries on regardless, ignoring the other's return, this feels like rejection. It hurts, and is also a missed opportunity for expressing love and gladness in each other. Besides, it's rude. We wouldn't treat guests like that. And isn't the one we chose as our life partner more important than a guest, who's here today and gone tomorrow? It's great that your partner has come safely home. Show them that you think so!

Do we still say a proper goodbye when we part in the mornings, if that is the pattern of our day? Nothing in life is guaranteed. Take an extra look. Have an extra kiss. I don't want to be morbid, but you never know what tomorrow will bring. Accidents happen. We can't afford to take anything for granted. My husband almost died of heart disease two years ago. It sharpened my appreciation of him enormously.

The little touches make such a difference. They cost so little, yet they give so much. If the greetings, pleases and thank yous have lapsed a bit in our marriage, let's try to sprinkle them through the day again. It's like salting food – it tastes better. And let's realise afresh just how important our partner is to us. It will help us to show more respect and thoughtfulness, and will give our partner that good feeling of being treasured and loved – and the more we are loved, the more lovable we become.

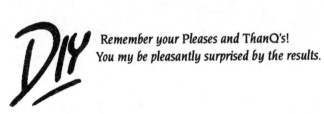

Remember your Pleases and ThanQ's!
You my be pleasantly surprised by the results.

Look After the Pennies...

Why is money so often an area of friction in our marriage? Is it because there isn't enough? Would a windfall from the Pools or the National Lottery solve all our problems? Or would we simply aim higher and end up with the same problems again on a bigger scale?

Philip and Natalie have two young children. Philip has a job that earns a reasonable wage, but not enough for Natalie's tastes. So Natalie earns extra money by doing some cooking and other part-time work. However, she spends everything she earns mostly on clothes and accessories for herself, and the family is soon struggling to make ends meet. The children need school uniforms and expensive shoes, the car insurance goes up, and Philip's salary just can't stretch that far.

Arguments become more and more heated as the stress increases, until finally Natalie walks out, taking the children with her, and goes back to Mum.

Philip and Natalie were not very good at talking through problems of any kind, so when it came to money, Philip accused her of extravagance, Natalie accused him of meanness and taunted him for earning such a poor wage, and they ended up shouting at each other. They didn't seem able to sit down and work out any sensible answers, whereas Guy and Juliet did.

Guy and Juliet's problem was different. Guy was made redundant, so they couldn't keep up the mortgage payments and had to hand the keys back to the building society, losing the share of the house they had already paid for. As if this were not bad enough, the house was resold at a loss by the building society, who then sent them a bill for £16,000, being the drop in price since the previous sale.

Stunned and shattered by this impossible demand, and with no means to pay, they sat down to work out what they could do. Guy got another job, Juliet found a weekend job, they rented accommodation, and had to pay child minders to look after their two little boys when they were both working at the same time. Gradually, they are managing to pay off their huge, unexpected debt.

They camp for holidays, and keep all their expenses to an absolute minimum. Juliet is very clever at creating tasty, wholesome meals out of nothing very much, and Guy has become a skilful handyman. They find bargains by keeping their eyes open – there's the basket of 'sell-by' items; the 'Help the Aged' and Sue Ryder shops offer some excellent clothes; local bric-a-brac stalls, boot sales and fêtes can yield some useful finds; January and Summer sales, and the 'Seconds' shelves where you can never find anything wrong with the clothes.

Somehow, although it's a real struggle, they're working it out between them, with family help from time to time. They review the position regularly, as well as sharing their worries.

Another reason for friction over money is today's very high expectations, even by newly-married couples. What used to be considered a luxury, something to save and wait for one day, is now thought essential from Day One. For example, a television, a car, a washing machine (and tumble drier?), even a dishwasher, a video, holidays abroad, a microwave, a three-piece suite, carpets throughout the house....

Perhaps one partner comes from a home where all these things are taken for granted, and the other has watched parents gradually acquire one item at a time, each arrival being greeted with real excitement and appreciation. I know a young couple who don't have a television or video, but do have a dishwasher. They don't have any fitted carpets, most of their furniture consists of family cast-offs, they have one car and a bike between them, but a beautiful new Aga. These happened to be their priorities.

Every couple is different, and lots of compromises will have to be made as we each sort out what we feel are 'musts' and then what is financially possible. Even 'musts' have to wait sometimes, but are all the more appreciated when they do appear.

Another possible cause of friction can come from entering into more long-term financial commitments than we can safely handle, leaving no funds in case of sudden need or crisis. In these circumstances, it's easy to blame our partner and get angry with each other.

Shortage of money, for any reason, can make us edgy. For instance, over the length of telephone calls, seemingly unnecessary car journeys, or too many lights being left on around the house. The partner with greater self-control – and with luck, a head for figures – is probably going to be the better one to hold the family purse-strings.

A 'saver' may marry a 'spender', and this too can cause problems.

Frances' family were never well off, but always generous. They would gladly give away a pair of boots or a cake or some cash to anyone in need, even when their own needs were considerable – yet somehow they always had enough to eat and were never cold through lack of clothes.

Giles' family budgeted very carefully. His parents sat down once a month and worked out exactly how their month's available money would be allocated.

When Frances and Giles married, they had a problem. Frances often gave away their next meal, or emptied her purse for a weeping caller, driving Giles to distraction because his budgeting was thrown into total disarray.

'We haven't got that money. You mustn't hand it out like sweets at the door. We needed that for the phone bill.'

'Oh, I'm sorry, Giles, but Amy was so desperate, her mum's got flu and she couldn't get to the shops…'

'Well, that's just their bad luck.'

'Giles, how heartless of you. How can you say that?'

'But don't you see, if we go on like this we're going to be in debt.'

'No, we're not. Anyway, we can always have beans on toast for supper. Now, don't worry so much.'

Amy gave Giles a kiss. 'You're great, darling, and I do think you're very wise, but my heart takes over from my head sometimes. So did Mum's, but we never starved.'

DIY Talk about your own family's financial habits and attitudes.
Discuss your views on 'essentials'. If possible, agree a list of priorities. Consult it when money becomes available.

'Buy Now – and Pay For It Later!'

The media shout at us to spend, spend, spend. With tantalising pictures, alluring voices and the ever-present word 'only' preceding a price of £9.99, £99.99 or £999.99, they use every subtle and not-so-subtle means at their disposal to persuade us to spend money we don't have on things we don't need. 'Buy now!' they say. 'Unrepeatable offer!' 'A unique opportunity!' 'Clearance Bargains!' 'Don't delay! Ring today!' 'You can't do without this fantastic, time-saving, space-saving miracle machine!' 'Order now for guaranteed next day delivery!'

What these advertisements seldom mention is the heavy interest charges for long-term repayment, the addition of fitting or delivery charges, VAT, and essential extras, for example, the mouse, mouse mat, printer, paper and discs for a PC. The hidden costs can mount up alarmingly and need to be checked before we sign on the dotted line.

We have to develop sales cynicism and sales resistance or we'll end up with a load of goods and a load of problems. All those mail-order catalogues that pour in through the letter box – it might be better to bin at least some of them without opening them. Resist the temptation to get the newest music centre or add too much to the collection of CDs or videos. It's not easy, but there are times when it *has* to be done.

As far as possible, let's try to ensure that the

sacrifices are about the same for each of us, unless one of us has been given to extravagance, in which case it's only fair that he or she makes the greater adjustment.

Sudden change of circumstance can cause desperate financial problems, as many have discovered during the recent recession. And it doesn't matter whether the family has been rich or poor, a sudden collapse of income is devastating. The threatened or actual loss of home, the fear of bankruptcy, the letters from creditors, the feeling of failure and shame that often accompany the situation, even if it's no one's fault at all, is a terrible blow to any family.

Justin had built up a small business, but at the height of the recession, he was forced to sell his share to his partner. He became another statistic on the unemployment register, but the sense of helplessness, hopelessness and worry was the worst part.

He had a wife and three children, and quite a big mortgage. He and Penny discussed the whole thing together. They talked to the Building Society about rescheduling the mortgage, and decided that she would look for part-time work while he job hunted. She managed to pick up some work, and Justin did any work he could find, from gardening to decorating or filling in for people on holiday. It's been a terrible struggle for the family, and some months they've only just been able to pay the bills, but Justin has managed to find a steadier job now, so things may look up.

Throughout the two-year crisis, Justin and Penny have worked together. They explained to the children what the situation was, and why they couldn't have lots of presents and holidays away, so they coped with it as a family, and they now say that it's brought them closer together than they were before the crisis began.

Other changes can also cause major financial difficulties. Severe illness in the family, an unexpected extra baby or a house move may tip a family over the edge if they are not extremely careful.

The rising cost of essentials such as insurance, petrol, train fares, the water bill, let alone children's sports or music equipment, uniform and shoes can be a nasty shock.

One family decided to have three separate accounts: a current account for normal needs, an emergency account for crises – eg. new cooker unexpectedly needed, burst pipes mean redecorating and new carpets, and a long-term savings account. They find this works really well for them, and prevents that dreadful sinking feeling when emergencies crop up – as they certainly do for all of us.

The key to solvency is how much we spend, not how much we earn. There may simply not be enough money to go round, but there are times when it's more a question of learning to live within the limits of our income. Some very poor families seem to manage, whereas families on higher incomes can come to grief.

It may help to agree a top limit that either can spend without consulting the other. On occasion it may be better to hire than to buy – for instance, just hire a television for the winter. It can be done, and it can be fun too, as the family does more things together, playing games or going for a stroll or a picnic and *talking,* instead of being glued to the box.

We need to avoid having too much month left over at the end of our money! A monthly budget is extremely helpful, and need not be complicated.

There is some very useful and simple computer software available which is designed for home budgeting.

Would it help to make use of this?

Before starting to create a budget, it's good to analyse what is happening with the available money at the moment. How much goes on monthly long-term payments? How much, if any, do we save? How much goes on food and drink, and what proportion of that is 'necessary' as opposed to 'luxury' or treats? We need to put specific amounts against these items, adding up the actual bills over a two or three-month period. Guesswork won't do – some wishful thinking may get wound into it!

When the lists are made and the sums are done, we can see better whether the income is going to cover the expenditure. If it looks unlikely, we will need to agree together what to delay or cut down on until we have a budget that is workable. If we face a big problem, we may decide to put away the credit card. Some people have even decided to cut up their card and operate on a 'cash only' basis. Cash envelopes for various needs – kept in a secure place – are an option. For instance, one for food, one for clothes, another for presents, etc. A money box for, say, the TV licence, Christmas, or car insurance, with every 50p coin going into it, could be useful.

One partner may be much more gifted at budgeting than the other, so perhaps they may agree that he or she deals with financial matters. This will mean that the rest of the family must go along with the one who's doing the job, or there will be major upsets. It's no good agreeing that the wife does the budget if the husband then regularly overspends, or the other way round. The couple need to talk it through and find a way that works for them.

Some men feel that it's essential that they are seen as

A Monthly Budget Planner

First, list all sources of income:

Earnings	_____
Child Benefit	_____
Other benefits	_____
Anything else?	_____
TOTAL	£_____

Then, list all known expenditure:

Mortgage	_____
N. Insurance	_____
Tax	_____
Pension payment	_____
Food	_____
Clothes	_____
Electricity	_____
Gas, oil, water	_____
Household needs	_____
Presents	_____
Saving for holiday	_____
Newspapers, books	_____
Pocket money	_____
Toiletries	_____
Charitable giving	_____
Car expenses	_____
Garden costs?	_____
Travel	_____
Sport, music	_____
Leisure activities	_____
Saving for Christmas, new furnishings, a rainy day.	_____
TOTAL	£_____

'the provider', so that when they can't do it as they would like, they get very depressed and down-hearted. This sort of man needs extra love and encouragement from his wife at such a time. In the same way, if the wife earns a bigger salary, she needs to be extremely sensitive in order not to downgrade her husband or make him feel inadequate. The money we have is our money. We are very grateful for it, and will do our best to share it out as the family needs it.

DIY Openness and honesty are vital in financial matters. As long as we can keep talking, we can cope. So dont be secretive! Be open! And keep talking!

Whatever the situation, both parents must feel free to dig into the family pot when needs arise. If the wife doesn't work, or if there is a 'house-husband' in the family, consider the enormous value of the non income-bearing role: caring for the children, cooking, cleaning, washing, ironing, gardening, DIY, home car maintenance, shopping, playing, reading. It would be extremely expensive to pay someone to do these things, and their importance in terms of family relation-ships is incalculable. Parents give their children love, care, security, identity and all the many essential and intangible things that every child needs every moment of its growing years. There are many child-minders, some of them admirable, but there are only two parents, and their contribution to their children's development is unique.

If a debt problem should arise, the important thing is to share it, yet there is a real reluctance to do this. The one whose situation or action has precipitated it may well be too ashamed to admit it, even if it is not their fault. But debt is our problem, not yours or mine, and we need to share it, talk about it, and seek to work through it together. If apologies are appropriate, then so is forgiveness. We all make mistakes. Anger, accusation and defensiveness won't solve anything but will drive us apart, which is far more damaging than the debt itself.

Owen came home one day very depressed.

'What's the matter?' asked Rachel.

'The garage has just rung. The car hasn't passed its MOT. They say it'll cost over £400 + VAT to get it up to scratch.'

'**£400!**' Rachel burst into tears. 'But it **can't** be that much – and we need the car. I can't get the children to school without it, and how will I do the shopping, and…".

'Didn't you notice the tyres were worn? And the exhaust's half off, apparently. And there's rust too…'.

'It's not for **me** to notice that kind of thing! A car is just a way of getting somewhere, as far as I'm concerned. Why didn't **you** notice?'

Owen wasn't listening. He was looking at the last bank statement. According to that, and their budget, they had about £39 in hand.

This conversation could end in several different ways. Owen and Rachel might have a flaming row, retire hurt and angry, and solve nothing. They might have a sob and a cuddle, and end up in a pity heap. Or they might start to discuss their situation and begin to work out a step-by-step plan of action to help themselves.

As long as we can keep talking, we have hope. Not even the worst financial crisis need drive us apart. On the contrary, our common problem can lead us to hang on even more tightly to each other as we face the storm together, and by hook or by crook we shall survive, and so will our marriage.

Flown the Nest?

When we are young, we are naturally dependent on our parents or whoever cares for us, but as we grow towards adulthood, these strong emotional ties gradually loosen so that we are ready for independence by the time we leave home. We finally let go when we marry, and our primary emotional tie becomes our partner, not our parents. Or does it?

The old mother-in-law jokes suggest otherwise.

'What do you do when you see your mother-in-law about to drive over a cliff in your new car?'

Some parents treat their offspring as children even when they are thirty, forty or fifty years old, demanding that they come home for Granny's birthday, or spend Christmas with them. One mother rang her son every single day for twenty years. A son kept his twenty-five-year-old marriage concealed from his mother for fear of her anger if she knew. A father wouldn't speak to his son because the son had decided to become an entertainer instead of having a 'sensible career'.

These things are extremely painful. We need to leave home not only physically but emotionally if our marriage is to be successful. We keep *contact* with our parents, we respect and honour them, but they no longer control us and our lives. The relationship needs to change to one of friendship between equals. That means that we don't 'run home to mum', nor does she tell us what to do. We are independent people. We've truly moved out of one home and relationship in order to move into another.

Then we are ready to 'cleave', as the old translation of the Bible said, to our partner. This means to stick like super-glue to each other, to be utterly and totally committed to one another. This commitment is what will carry us through the early months, the changes when children come, and the low times in our lives when the going's tough and the odds seem against us.

Roy and Mandie had a difficult year. They took in a lodger to help make ends meet, and the lodger found Mandie rather attractive. Roy was at work all day, the children were one and three years old, and the lodger only had a part-time job. The lodger started standing very close to Mandie when she was cooking, and caressing her when she was changing the baby's nappies.

Mandie was flattered at first, and then she realised where it could lead. She thought how hurt Roy would be, how happy they'd been, and how much she loved the children. She decided to tell him.

'I don't know what to do,' she finished. 'We need the money, but I'm afraid he'll go too far, and I don't want...'

'Thank you, love, for telling me. I knew something was going on. Leave it to me. I'll deal with it.'

Mandie hugged Roy. 'I'm sorry,' she said. 'You know it's you I really love.'

'Yes, I do, and we're not going to let this come between us, are we?'

Roy and Mandie got through their rough patch. They stuck together and made it.

Charlie and Kate, were faced with a different problem. Their second baby, a little girl, was born with a congenital heart defect and only lived for five days.

Of course everything at home was ready for the new baby. The cot was prepared, toys were scattered about, baby clothes and nappies were in the drawer, the pram in the porch. Kate came home from hospital and cried and cried, but Charlie didn't say a word. He got the loft ladder down and collected all the baby things – everything – and put them up in the loft out of sight. It was as if he hoped that by hiding all the evidence he could shut out the

experience and, with it, the pain and the grief. For Kate, the effect was devastating, but whenever she cried, Charlie told her 'not to be silly'. Without the toys and baby clothes she couldn't grieve for her little daughter as she needed

Whatever happens, stick together like glue!

to, but Charlie just tried to shut it out.

The two of them had very different temperaments. Their way of coping with grief was as different as they were. But they clung to each other nevertheless, not only for their own sake, but for the sake of their three-year-old, and they made it. They now have two more lovely children and understand each other much better.

Sticking together in a crisis is so important. It could be grief, illness, a house move, redundancy, the death of a parent, an accident. We all cope with crises in our own way, but we need to talk about it together and hang on to each other tight as we weather the storm. We need each other more now than when things are swimming along, for unless we're careful, we can be driven apart not together, because of the different way we cope with crisis. No way is 'right' or 'wrong'. Each way is valid. As we face and come through painful times together, we find our love growing stronger and deeper. No one is immune from problems and troubles. It's what we do with them that matters. They can become building blocks, strengthening our marriage, or dividing walls that alienate us and drive us apart.

Have you ever stuck two pieces of card together, then changed your mind and tried to pull them apart? What happened? Probably both pieces were badly damaged and torn.

The same thing happens when a married couple pull apart from each other. Both partners are severely damaged and torn. Sticking together can be very hard, but tearing ourselves apart is often a lot more painful.

DIY

Think. Are you friends with your parents or are they still to some extent controlling you? What can you do to become friends instead of 'the children'? Determine to stick together like glue, whatever happens. Your commitment will see you through.

Family First

What comes top of your list? Your job? Your wife? Your husband? Your children? Your dog? Voluntary work? Home and garden? Sport? Keeping fit? Money? The car? These days, most people are just glad they've got a job. But for some, there are choices to be made. Is it worth the sacrifice of family time and happiness to earn more money? If the money is for essentials – the mortgage, food, clothes, running the car – then we have no choice. But for some there is a choice. The extra money may go on a video or fax machine, a new car, pricey presents for the children, extravagant holidays, expensive sport and entertaining. There's nothing wrong with any of these things, but if earning the money to pay for them comes between us and our partner and children, and stops us from spending time together, are we all going to be 'better off' in the end?

Bill had a well-paid job that involved long hours away from home, commuting before the children were awake, returning when they were in bed, and only seeing his family at weekends. When he was home, everyone and everything clamoured for his attention. The children wanted him to play. The lawn needed mowing. Elaine, his wife, longed to talk with him. There were repairs to do in the house. The car was dirty. He didn't know where to start, and then suddenly it was Sunday night and another week was about to begin.

Then he was made redundant. At first the shock was terrible, but he was given six months' pay which cushioned the financial burden and gave him time to look for another job.

Being one of the lucky ones, he found a job about three months later, although it was at a considerably lower salary. It was also fairly local, so it only took twenty-five minutes to get there each day, which meant a later start and an earlier return home.

'It's so much nicer having you home more,' said Elaine one evening. 'The children are loving it. They look forward to your coming every evening and get really excited.'

'I'm enjoying it too, but I'm afraid we shan't be able to have a holiday abroad this summer.'

'Never mind, we can have just as much fun in Devon or Cornwall. I'd far rather have you around more, and have time to talk and to do things at weekends.'

'Yes. If someone had said three months ago that I'd be happier with less money, I'd never have believed them, but it's true. I wouldn't go back to the old job for anything!'

Would you rather have a bigger bank balance or a home full of laughter? Of course, both would be nice, but we sometimes have to choose one or the other. Would you rather play golf every Saturday or take the family on an outing? Which would you choose, a game of cricket with your son in the garden or the park, or some business phone calls?

One wife was asked, 'When did your husband stop playing hockey every Saturday afternoon?'

'When I threw a saucepan at him!' she replied.

If your wife has been looking after your children all week, isn't it time for her to have a break and some fun? Or if your husband stays at home to look after the children, the same applies. How would you feel if every Saturday afternoon was more of what you'd been doing from Monday to Friday – and without pay?

In the end, what matters to you most? Is it your job or your marriage or your sport or your reputation in the community? What could you do without, and what would be unthinkable to lose?

Our choices reflect our priorities. We may be able to choose to get home early and see the children, or have a beer with a friend after work. We may choose to bake a birthday cake, visit a neighbour, mend Sarah's doll or watch TV. We can spend money on buying things, or pay for a baby-sitter and go out for a meal together.

Let's face it. Someone else could probably do our job. We can manage with the old car. But nobody else in all the world can take the place of our partner, or be father or mother to our children. To these people, we are indispensable. We're the only one they have. If we blow it, they've had it, and the pain and damage that both we and they will suffer is incalculable. And with our children, we'll never get a second chance. No rerun of this video. It's now – or never.

DIY What are your priorities at the moment, between your work, your partner, your children and your other activities? Write them down if possible. (Would your family agree with what you've said?)
What choices could you both make to give your marriage a higher priority? Are you willing to make them?

A Questionnaire on Our Families

Settle down one evening or weekend and do the following questionnaire together. You may discover all sorts of interesting things about each other!

In my family: **Yes/No?**

1. Punctuality was important. ☐
2. Dad always dealt with money matters. ☐
3. Holiday plans were discussed by everyone. ☐
4. The house was always clean and tidy. ☐
5. People often turned up unexpectedly. ☐
6. We had to wear slippers in the house. ☐
7. Dad did the garden and Mum cleaned the house. ☐
8. Mum disciplined the children. ☐
9. We hugged each other lots. ☐
10. We were only allowed one hour of TV a day. ☐
11. We had to make our beds and clean our rooms. ☐
12. Mum and Dad often argued. ☐
13. We had two dogs and a cat. ☐
14. We always went to the country for the summer holidays. ☐
15. We took it in turns to wash up. ☐

Just Be There

Sylvia was putting the kettle on and sobbing her heart out. She and Barry had heard from their married daughter that morning that the baby she was carrying was severely handicapped. The other children were desperately upset, and so were they. The hospital had suggested an abortion, but they had decided against it. 'We can't play God,' they said. 'We just can't do it.' So the next five months were going to be for them all an agonising time of waiting.

Barry went to work as usual, but Sylvia wasn't due to work that day, so she spent the time doing chores and weeping. When Barry came home, he walked into the kitchen and found her, red-eyed and weary. He put an arm round her, gave her a kiss, and pulled out his handkerchief to mop up her tears.

'Cheer up, love. There's nothing we can do about it, and you'll just exhaust yourself by crying. Let's have a cup of tea and you'll feel better.'

Sylvia mopped her tears as best she could, and set the tray, but the sobs began again.

'What is it, dear? Can I do anything?' asked Barry, bewildered.

'No, just be there,' sobbed Sylvia. 'Hold me and give me time...'

That's it. 'Just be there…hold me…give me time.' To many men, a 'good cry' seems a contradiction in terms. How can crying be 'good'? Yet that's exactly what his wife may need.

Have you ever been stopped in the middle of a yawn? If so, you'll know that in a short time, you'll be needing to have another one. Stopping someone when they haven't finished crying has much the same effect. It simply means that they will soon need to weep again.

The best way that a man can help is by lovingly holding his wife and patiently waiting, without words, until she calms down. Then he can offer words of comfort and sympathy, and finally they can begin to talk through the distress that caused it.

When I'm upset, for whatever reason, the first thing I

need is sympathy, a hug, understanding, a kiss and a cuddle. Only then is it helpful to begin to analyse the situation or to ask why. Because my husband tends to be more rational and less emotional, his first response is often: 'Now whatever made you feel like this? Is it the time of the month, or have you been doing too much? Perhaps you're over-tired.' Or worse still: 'It's a glorious day. How can you possibly be unhappy?'

The natural response of most men to painful situations is to want to solve the problem, to do something, to fix it. If nothing can be done, they may react by trying to push the problem aside or by seeking to minimise it. 'It's not really that bad' or 'Lots of people have to cope with worse situations than this.'

These responses don't help. The first response must be loving sympathy.

A woman usually *feels* a painful situation acutely, and is not too concerned – yet – about *fixing* it. She enters deeply into the situation with her emotions, and it is only on this level that she can be genuinely comforted.

When our baby grandchild died recently, she was the second baby from the same family to die. We had a simple funeral in the country church where her brother was buried, and then the second little white coffin was lowered beside the first.

When everyone had gone, and it was dark outside, I walked into the night and wept aloud. After a while, my husband heard me and came out. He said nothing, but held me in his arms and let me continue until the sobs died down and I was ready to go back indoors. That was comfort. He made no attempt to cheer me up, no unnecessary comment, no comment at all, in fact. He just stood there and held me. He let me blurt out how hard I was finding it. He was *there*. That's what I needed, and it was enough.

Comfort, true comfort, is coming alongside someone, being where they are, feeling what they're feeling, sharing their hurt or grief or disappointment – and that's all!

Very often, there is no 'solution'. If someone dies, or you lose your job, or a dear friend gets terminal cancer, 'solutions' don't exist. Mr Fix-it has nothing he can do. But he can offer comfort, and comfort is healing in itself. It may not be a quick fix. That depends on the degree of pain. But being there, and sharing it, allows the healing process to begin.

Mrs Feel-it isn't the only one who needs comfort. Mr Fix-it may give the impression that he has no needs, but we all need someone to be there when we're distressed.

Clive came home bitterly disappointed that he hadn't been given the promotion he was expecting. He burst in, banged the door, threw his coat and bag down, and poured himself a beer.

Sandra knew that something must be wrong and came to find him.

'Had a bad day?' she asked kindly.

'Bad day! I'll say I had a bad day! Adrian's been promoted instead of me, and I'm just left in limbo. How can they do that to me? Haven't I worked long enough hours for them, giving up my weekends?'

Clive was angry, but under the anger, he was deeply hurt.

'I'm so sorry, love,' said Sandra, putting an arm round his shoulder. 'How terribly disappointing for you, and it's so hard that Adrian's got promotion when he joined after you. I'm so sorry.'

Clive's anger began to subside. He put his head in his hands. Sandra sat beside him and gave him the occasional squeeze.

It was what he needed, for her to be there, and slowly he began to feel comforted.

An independent-minded wife may hide her emotions, but the fact is that she needs to share them too, just like the rest of us.

Angela went to collect her two young children from the child-minder one day, and found her baby son, Danny, in the child-minder's arms.

'He's a bit feverish, Mrs Reed. He's been fretful all day. Probably teething.'

Angela went to take him and he burst out crying, hanging onto the child-minder. She had to prise his little hands off her sweater and hand him over, screaming, to Angela.

Angela took the children home, put them to bed, and began to cook supper, flying round the kitchen at double speed. Hugh came in, heard the noise, and found a white-faced Angela at the sink.

'What's up, love?' he asked.

'Oh nothing,' she said. 'Supper'll be ready soon.'

She turned the TV up rather loud while they ate, but when they sat down with a cup of coffee, Hugh turned it off and sat very close to Angela.

'There is something the matter, isn't there? Is it to do with work?'

'No.'

'The children?'

'Well, yes.' Then she told him what had happened with Danny.

'He doesn't love me,' she concluded. 'He loves her best. I'm his mum, and I leave him every day, and now he doesn't want me!'

Hugh listened, and lent her his handkerchief, and held

her hand. He was there.

By the time she'd finished telling him how she felt, Angela already felt a bit better. A little while later, they began to look at the whole situation, and discuss what could be done.

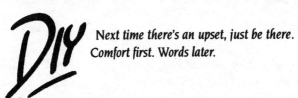

*Next time there's an upset, just be there.
Comfort first. Words later.*

Babies Don't Rule OK!

Will and Debbie came home from the hospital glowing with the happiness and wonder of their first baby, a beautiful eight-pounder they had named Emma Jane. She lay asleep in the new baby-seat in the front of the car as they drove home, and Debbie's mum was there to greet them at the door. It was smiles all round as Emma was carefully taken upstairs to her own room with the Noah's Ark frieze round the walls, a teddy-bear mobile, and the large furry rabbit waiting on the chair.

'I can't believe it. It's just so wonderful!' said Debbie.

'She's the loveliest baby, isn't she?' agreed her mum.

'And you've made me a daddy, haven't you?' cooed Will as he stroked her soft cheek.

They left her there to go and unpack the car, and immediately she began to wail.

'Oh dear, I'd better feed her,' said Debbie, and she picked her up and took her to the living room which was warm and cosy.

Debbie was tired, and after putting Emma down again, she curled up in bed for a rest. An hour later, just as they settled down to a meal together, Emma started to cry again.

'Bother, she can't be hungry, but I suppose I'd better see,' said Debbie, and off she went.

There was soon silence from the cradle, and Debbie

came back to eat her lunch. But five minutes later, Emma started again.

'Oh dear, I wonder what's the matter now,' said Debbie, getting up again.

'I should leave her for a little while,' advised her mum. 'She's fed and winded and dry, and she's not too hot or too cold. I think she just fancies some company. If you run to her every time she murmurs, you won't have a moment's peace.'

But Debbie couldn't sit still. She was up again, and soon returned with Emma in her arms. Within two minutes she was quiet, and Debbie finished her lunch single-handed.

The night hardly seemed to happen and yet it seemed to last for ever. Emma woke up every one and a half to two hours, demanding something. They weren't sure whether it was food she wanted, or a dry nappy, or less coverings, or a cuddle...but she woke them anyway.

After a week, Will and Debbie were exhausted. Will could hardly drag himself off to work, and Debbie fell asleep at the kitchen table or any time she was able to sit down for five minutes.

Mum tried to help.

'Why not leave her a bit longer before you go to her, dear? She's perfectly all right. She'll probably settle in a short time if you give her a chance. You won't have much life of your own if you're always running to her. Anyway, crying's good exercise!' she added with a smile.

'But she might have a tummy ache, Mum, or be hungry or dirty. I can't leave her crying.'

'Well, you survived! I had the other two to look after, so you just had to take your turn. Half the time you'd gone to sleep again before I had time to attend to you. Babies are knowing little things, and she'll twist you round her little baby finger if you're not careful.'

After two weeks, Mum went home, and Debbie was on her own with all the usual chores – plus Emma.

Will would come home in the evening, and instead of a kiss and a cuddle at the door, he'd find Debbie feeding, changing or simply holding the baby, and the most he got was a quick 'Hello, love,' and a peck on the cheek.

Bedtime came, and Emma's 'last' feed didn't finish till around 11 pm. Then Debbie crashed into bed exhausted. Will was longing to cuddle up close to her,

to feel her warm body beside him again, and to make love. But she shrugged him off.

'Not now, Will. I'm too tired.'

After several weeks of this, Will began to get desperate.

'When is "now" going to come?' he asked one night when she was putting him off yet again. 'It's all very well, this baby business, but you're my wife, and I love you.'

'But I've been busy all day with Emma, and I just don't have the energy.'

'Emma, Emma, Emma! Everything's Emma these days. "I must feed Emma." "I must change Emma." "I must check Emma." Where do I fit in? – or perhaps I don't any more?'

'How can you be so selfish? Can't you see how tired I am? A baby's a full-time job, you know, and after all, she's your baby as well as mine. Don't you love her?'

'Yes, of course I love her, but I don't see why I've got to lose you. Can't you sometimes switch off from Emma and switch on to me?'

Now Debbie was upset too. 'You try looking after a baby twenty-four hours a day, seven days a week, then you'd understand.' And she turned her back to Will and went to sleep, leaving him sad and lonely in the dark.

A few days later, he tried again.

'Let's go and have a drink at the pub tonight. I'm sure Lena would pop in from next door and baby-sit for an hour.'

'What, leave Emma here with a stranger? We can't do that!' Debbie was horrified.

'Why ever not? Thousands of couples do it every day, and the children don't come to any harm. What could possibly happen to Emma in an hour? She'll be asleep anyway.'

'Oh no, Will. I couldn't leave her. I suppose we could take her with us.'

Will's voice rose in irritation. 'I don't want her with us. I want us to have just one hour on our own, the way it used to be. Please, love.'

'I'm sorry, Will, but I really can't leave her.'

A look of deep disappointment, hurt and pain crossed Will's face. 'OK. I'll go alone,' he said sadly, and walked slowly out through the door.

Soon afterwards, Debbie bumped into a friend outside the supermarket and they started talking.

'How's it going?' asked Jean. 'Everything OK?'

Debbie started the usual answer. 'Fine, thanks. Emma's lovely…' but Jean noticed a slight hesitation, and they were good friends, so she pressed the point.

'Any problems?'

'Well, it's Will. He's so irritable nowadays, and he takes hardly any notice of Emma. He wants me to go out for a drink, and when I say I can't leave Emma he gets almost angry. I don't know what's come over him.'

'Why don't you get a baby-sitter?'

'But I couldn't.'

'Why not?'

'Well, I just couldn't.'

Jean became serious. 'You *must,*' she said. 'You married Will, not Emma, and Will comes first.'

'But Emma needs me, and…'.

'So does Will, Debbie, and you must put him first. After all, if you two aren't happy, it'll make Emma miserable. You owe it to Emma to give Will time. He needs you just as much as Emma does.'

At last Jean seemed to be getting through.

'Do you really think so?'

'I know it, because Bob and I had the same problem.

I let the boys come first, and never realised how little I was giving him – of my time and affection and laughter, even smiles, let alone sex. Then his Dad and Mum offered to have the boys for a whole week so that we could go away. I didn't want to go but Bob insisted – and on holiday it all came out. How hurt he felt and how much he'd missed me. He'd felt really jealous of the boys, and all the love and time I gave them. He was very unhappy and beginning to wonder if he had a place in my life any more.

'I was shattered. I had no idea how he'd been feeling. We talked it all through, and worked out some changes we could make so that I became less tired, and we had time on our own. As the week went by, we began to cuddle again, and by the end, it was like a second honeymoon.'

Debbie felt challenged. She realised that she had to change her attitude. It wouldn't be easy, but suddenly she'd seen what she was doing to Will by putting Emma first. Before even unloading the shopping she decided to do something that she knew would please Will. She went next door and asked Lena if she'd baby-sit that evening.

'Of course I will. No problem. Any time.'

When Will came in, Debbie went straight to him and gave him a hug. He was amazed.

'I've asked Lena to come and baby-sit so that we can go out tonight,' she told him.

'That's fantastic! Great!' said Will. 'How long can she come for?'

'As long as we like, I think.'

'Brilliant! Let's have a drink *and* dinner!'

'But…'.

'No. No "buts" tonight Debbie,' said Will. 'This is a

celebration!' And he rang to book a table.

As they lay in bed that night, Debbie moved in closer to Will.

'I'm sorry,' she said. 'I didn't realise how much I'd cut you out.'

'And I don't think I've given you all the help I could either. Is there anything I could do to relieve you a bit?'

'Well, if you gave her a cuddle sometimes while I cooked the tea, it'd be great.'

'Right. I'll have a go, if Emma will let me!'

Will drew Debbie to him and tenderly began to make love to her. She knew she was forgiven.

Emma's great, she thought to herself, 'but she's going to have to learn that her Daddy is the greatest!'

DIY

Remember – Babies don't rule, OK?!
Discuss: Who calls the tune in your home? If it's the children, change channels! The best gift we can give our children is two loving parents.

'All Work and No Play...'

Martin and Lena were hard at work decorating the living room. Martin didn't really like the wallpaper that Lena had bought so triumphantly in the sale, and it was difficult to match up the pattern.

'This beastly stuff just won't come right,' he complained crossly. 'Why couldn't you have chosen something easier?'

'Well, I liked the colour, and it was down to half-price too. Think how much we've saved!'

'Just at the moment, I don't care how much we've saved. I'm fed up with the whole thing.'

At that moment, Dottie the dog barked in the garden and they both looked out of the window.

'The sun's come out,' said Lena. 'Come on! Let's leave this and go for a picnic in the forest, by that lovely stream. I expect the bluebells are out in the woods by now.'

'Brilliant idea!' said Martin, getting down off the step ladder. 'I'll get a rug and do Dottie's dinner while you put the food together for us.'

Within twenty minutes, everything was ready, Dottie jumped in the back of the car, panting happily, and off they set.

'This is fun!' smiled Lena as they drove along. 'It's ages since we had a bluebell picnic.'

They had a very happy afternoon, lying among the

bluebells, playing with Dottie in the stream, having their picnic and chasing each other, barefoot and laughing, through the damp, fresh grass, with Dottie barking at their heals.

'That was a great idea,' said Martin as they drove home. 'Let's do it again.'

Have you had any fun lately? Life has become so serious, so busy, so stressful, it often seems as if we don't have time to enjoy ourselves and have fun.

Children know better. They're always on the look out for fun. They play and enjoy themselves, giggle and chase each other. 'Ah yes,' we say, 'they've got plenty of time.' True, but if we have no time for fun, surely there must be something wrong somewhere? Everyone needs some fun, whether they're seven or seventy-seven. No family, no couple, should be so busy that they never do anything for fun.

A couple who were both on their second marriage, went on a marriage refresher weekend. When they married, they hadn't gone on honeymoon at all, thinking that it would upset the children if they went away too soon. During the weekend the subject of fun came up, and they suddenly recognised the missing ingredient in their relationship – fun! They had tried so hard to do what seemed best for the children that they hadn't given themselves any time for enjoyment together. They went home determined to make time for fun.

We can have so much fun as long as we allow time for it, and while we have fun, we get to know each other more, we learn to relate, we build our sense of togetherness and oneness, and we build in memories for the future.

What about a game of tennis or golf, a bike ride, a few days walking in the Lake District or climbing in the Highlands of Scotland, hiring an amusing video on a winter's night, fish and chips on the sea front, going to a film or a disco with friends, a swim, sharing an ice-cream in the park, or a walk on a wild and windy day? It doesn't really matter what we do as long as we both enjoy doing it and do it together.

Sue was full of complaints one Sunday evening.

'Monday tomorrow. You'll be gone by 7.30 am, leaving me all alone with three kids all day. I've got the biggest, smelliest pile of washing you ever saw, after our muddy walk today, and Peter can't go to nursery school. He's got a runny nose, and they're so strict about things like that. "It's not fair on the others," they'll say, so I'll have the whole lot round my feet. Johnny's always making Beth cry, he won't leave her alone, and if I tick him off he goes and messes up Peter's Lego and Peter gets all upset...'.

David listened, and thought how much quieter it would be for him in the office than for Sue at home.

'Tell you what,' he said. 'You know that kind lady from the church, the one who's recently moved into No. 14? She said to me only last week, "If ever you want to go out together, I'd be very happy to look after the children for a day. I miss my grandchildren so much now I'm living so far away from them. I'd really enjoy having some children again."'

'She can't have meant it,' said Sue doubtfully.

'Oh yes, she did. I'm going to go round and see her right now, and see if I can fix up something.'

David was back in ten minutes, grinning broadly.

'Her name's Janet, and she says she'll have them next Saturday! She seemed pleased to be asked. She'll come and see you during the week to meet the children, and you can show her where things are. Then we can go out for the day! Isn't that great?'

Sue cheered up as she gradually took in the amazing prospect of a whole day with David and without the children.

'It's almost too good to be true!' she said. 'Where shall we go? What shall we do?'

'Leave it to me,' said David. 'It'll be a surprise from start to finish.' He gave Sue a kiss. 'You'll enjoy every moment, I guarantee.'

She kissed him back. 'I can hardly wait!' she said.

David and Sue had a wonderful day, and came home feeling as if they'd been away for ages. Janet had enjoyed her day too, and the children were happy and full of all the things they'd done.

We are in danger of becoming bored and boring if we never do anything just for the fun of it. Could it be that shorter working hours and a bit less money would be a good exchange for a bit more fun and enjoyment together?

DIY

Have a brain-storming session. Each write a list of the things you enjoy doing. Find some that appeal to both of you, and fix a few dates for doing them. Have fun!

When Two Into One Won't Go

An expert in the field of marriage has said that there is a built-in tendency towards isolation in every marriage. We should consciously make choices, little ones as well as big ones, that bring us together and keep us close to each other. For we can slowly but surely slip from the early days of sharing and intimacy towards a relationship that could better be described as 'married singles' than a married couple.

William and Debbie are both professional people. William is a consultant physician, and Debbie is a full-time physiotherapist working in a hospital department. They have three young children, and a series of child-minders and cleaners with whom they juggle the household and child-minding responsibilities. The children are sometimes not sure who will pick them up or put them to bed or take them to gym class or piano lessons, and if one of them is ill, the organisation becomes a nightmare. The weekend is a constant tug of war between a mountain of post and domestic chores, the children's clamour for attention, the need for rest after the pressures of the week, and the need for William and Debbie simply to have time alone together.

Is this what we imagined marriage and family life to be like? William and Debbie say they find it very hard work, but don't really see any alternative. They love each other, but they are living largely separate lives.

Having two full-time careers outside the home is one way in which a couple can become more like 'married singles' than a married couple. 'We pass like ships in the night,' said another couple who have to work shifts in order to make ends meet. 'We're in danger of becoming strangers living in the same house.' A nurse said of her marriage: 'We exchange pleasantries, that's all.'

Even our own individual choices can lead to gradual isolation. He chooses to go to a Keep Fit class and join a choir. She chooses to join a committee and the bridge club. This means that for four evenings a week one partner may be in alone, and only one 'extra' needs to crop up for us not to have even one evening together.

Then of course there are the children. It is wonderful to have children, but there's no doubt that they require a great deal of our time and energy, from birth until they leave home. This means less time for each other, and calls for even greater determination on our part to write into the diary some firm, unbreakable engagements for us two.

We said goodbye to our youngest a few days ago. Nineteen, and off for five months, but effectively leaving home for good, apart from visits. Weeping on the way home, I was deeply grateful that my husband and I are good friends. How tragic it would be to see our last child leave home, turn to one another, and find we were strangers with nothing to say.

Another factor that drives us unwillingly towards singleness is the situation at work. Some employers treat their staff like disposable gloves. They use them flat out until they wear out, then get rid of them and employ someone else.

Work pressure today is enormous. Managers often ignore the fact that those who work for them are human beings, with a family and a home, and limited human resources. There are thousands of fathers – and a number of mothers – who hardly see their children to speak to except at weekends or on holidays. And many parents are too tired by the time they get home to talk together or take an interest in each other's day, whether they've both been out to work or not. Yet both of them need to unload and unwind.

Anthony is a solicitor. Fiona is a full-time mum with three children under school age and a fourth on the way. They went to a marriage weekend, and suddenly saw clearly that the pressures of his job and her looking after three children were driving them apart. They never had any time to themselves.

During the weekend, Anthony decided to pull out of three fairly demanding committees and responsibilities in order to have more time with Fiona and the children. A year later, Fiona said, 'I don't know how we'd have coped otherwise, especially with the baby. It took Anthony a lot of courage, but it was well worth it. We feel so much closer now.'

Other things keep us apart too. Clubs, meetings, church commitments, social life (if there's time for it!) and duties towards elderly relatives. Even our home lifestyle can conspire to keep us apart. We get busy in different parts of the house, or one in the garden and one in the garage, so there's no chance to talk. Husbands can be driven spare by a wife who spends all evening chatting to her friends on the telephone, and wives can be frustrated and hurt by a partner who appears to be obsessed with his vintage car or personal computer, or sits glued to the TV and won't say anything.

But did any of us marry just to share a fridge and a lawn-mower? Wasn't there at one time love and affection in our relationship, and a desire for companionship? Yes, there was – and there still is. We are longing for it so much that it hurts at times, but how can we find more 'together time'? How can we stop the creeping separateness, and stay friends and lovers?

The very first step is to acknowledge that there is a problem. As it is often women who crave relationship, they are more likely to be aware of the growing isolation in the marriage. Helping husbands to become aware and to see the need for change is not always easy, but it's vital. The very fact that his wife isn't happy and wants more of his company should alert him to the need for action.

Once both partners acknowledge that the present

state of affairs it not the best, they can begin to work out what changes they could make in order to have more time together. Sacrifices will probably have to be made on both sides. That's only fair. A committee may have to go; Keep Fit may have to give way to something that you both enjoy and can do together; perhaps one evening could become a home video time, or a special meal time.

What about some regular early nights to allow time for love-making? (Lock the door first, and put on the ansaphone if you have one!) The possibilities are endless. Only the will is needed, and once the new pattern is gradually established, the renewing of friendship and closeness together is worth everything.

It might help to ask ourselves: Do we feel secure in each other's love, even though we seldom get the chance to meet and communicate? What about spending half an hour on a quiet evening, after the children are in bed, or going for a walk so that we can talk this through? We could ask each other, 'Do you feel secure in my love?' 'Do I feel secure in your love?' 'Can we trust each other completely?'

If the answer for either of us is: 'I'm not sure', it's time we seriously considered making changes if it's at all possible. So many marriages die of starvation. If we can keep ours well fed, we shall be doing ourselves and our family a very good turn.

Those who marry and live happily ever after have learned to feed their love and go on feeding it. What gain is it to us if we make £1000 more each year, get to the top, have lots of friends and serve our community loyally, yet lose touch with our partner? Money can't buy the most precious things in the world. The fulfilment of shared love, joyful laughter among parents and children, open affection and unselfish caring, the wonderful security of being deeply loved – these things are beyond price. They cost time, effort, determination, stickability, planning and self-sacrifice – all of these and more. But the rewards are far greater than the effort and far richer than gold.

Some of us are forced into a 'married singles' lifestyle, at least for a while, but as soon as we can we need to make changes. There are so many pitfalls in living together yet apart, whereas the sharing of ourselves in true marriage and oneness can be an experience of ever-increasing satisfaction, security and enormous joy as the decades roll by.

DIY

Think: Are we in danger of being 'married singles'?
What changes can we make? And how soon can we make them?

Love Is also Friendship

Are you both lovers and good friends as well? Even best friends? How often do you manage to do something together that you both enjoy?

Caroline turned over sleepily.

'D'you realise, we've got the whole day to ourselves today, for the first time in two and a half years? Mum's not bringing Tom home till his bed-time.'

Tony reached across under the duvet and pulled her closer.

'Mmmm, what a treat. Let's think what we'd like to do.'

They lay there cuddling and sharing ideas.

'Go to that lovely old pub and have scampi and chips and a Capuccino.'

'Go and choose a new carpet for the stairs and bring it home with us.'

'See that film we've been longing to go to.'

'Stay in bed all day, make love and read and eat breakfast every few hours.'

'Visit a Spring garden and have a cream tea.'

'OK. What's your best idea?' asked Tony.

'Garden and cream tea,' said Caroline. 'What's yours?'

'Breakfast in bed, choose a carpet, and lunch at the pub.'

'Well, that works fine! We can have breakfast, go and

look for a carpet, have a pub lunch, then go to a garden and finish up with a cream tea.'

'Great! I'll go and get breakfast.'

'No, you won't. You always have to do it. Let me have a go.'

Caroline grinned doubtfully at Tony, who was not very practical.

'Let's do it together,' she suggested.

They had a wonderful day, and came back full of fresh air and delicious food.

'That was such fun! Let's do it again soon!' said Caroline with a happy grin.

Tony and Caroline enjoyed their day enormously. Others choose differently if they have some special time together.

One couple may like to get a take-away curry and watch their favourite television programme together. Another may like to drive to the sea and take a stroll along the front. Others enjoy gardening together, or going for walks in the country. Some like doing the decorating together; others prefer to go to a health club or like reading by the fire on a winter's evening. There's great companionship in silence as well as talking. To sit in a room with a friend, each absorbed in a book or magazine, can be a very peaceful and satisfying experience.

Think of a special activity you've shared: steak and chips while you watch a video, visiting a historic house or garden, breakfast in bed on Sunday morning. When did you last do that enjoyable thing together? Christopher Robin and Pooh were friends:

So wherever I am, there's always Pooh,
There's always Pooh and Me.
'What would I do?' I said to Pooh.
'If it wasn't for you,' and Pooh said: 'True,
It isn't much fun for One, but Two
Can stick together,' says Pooh, says he.
'That's how it is,' says Pooh.

From Us Two by A.A. Milne.

Friends can become better friends, but they can also lose touch.

Geoff and Louise had been married for ten years. They had three small boys, and Louise had given up her job to be a full-time mum, while Geoff worked for a computer company.

Before the children came, they often used to go out together for a meal or a drive. They liked films too, and had great fun planning their small garden and wall-papering the bedrooms.

When the boys arrived, Louise's time was taken up more and more with looking after them and doing the household chores. They couldn't afford to get a baby sitter very often, and their parents lived too far away, so they went out less and less.

Geoff did the garden in the evenings on his own. Louise was either too busy or too tired to help him. When Geoff felt like having a cuddle and making love, Louise pushed him off. 'I'm too tired,' she said. 'I don't feel like it.'

They didn't seem to get time for any real conversation together. One of the boys was always around or interruptions came from the phone or the neighbours. Geoff withdrew increasingly into his work, and said little. He gave up trying to show his love for Louise. She didn't seem to want it. Louise grew more and more weary and depressed. She let her hair get messy and didn't bother about her clothes. She ate for comfort and gained two stone.

Then one day, Geoff didn't come home. He'd given up and gone back to mum. No other girl was involved, but the utter loneliness was more than he could take.

Louise realised then how completely they'd lost touch. She hadn't even known how Geoff was feeling, and he wasn't aware of her unhappiness either, because they hadn't talked to each other properly for over two years. And now it was too late.

Suppose a young couple buy a new car and drive it home with great pride and pleasure. But it lives in the road outside their house, and soon the dirt of passing traffic, and the rain, takes some of the shine off. The children leave junk on the floor, and no one gives it a good wash. Rust develops, and after a year that smart new car has lots its glamour. Why? Not because there was anything wrong with it, but simply through neglect. No one looked after it, so it deteriorated.

Dr David Ferguson of the Centre for Marriage and Family Intimacy, Austin, Texas, says, 'The best marriages are those that are worked at.'

Friendship is like that car. It needs attention, care, running repairs – apologies, explanations, regular use and a 'top up', such as a special meal or fun time – to keep it in good working order. We arrange the necessary services for the car, the mower and the washing-machine. We repaint our walls and repair leaking windows. We hang new curtains and vacuum the carpets. Yet we do nothing for our own most treasured possession – our marriage, our friendship. That friendship is alive, but it can't stay that way unless we look after it. Let's do all we can to help it to thrive.

Like Geoff and Louise, we can lose touch with someone who lives under the same roof. Friendship is a living organism, constantly changing, growing or dying, thriving or starving, according to the care and attention it gets. To stay friends we need to go on doing the things friends do: share our interests, spend time on ourselves, care for each other and not take each other for granted. A common roof doesn't guarantee a common life. It is no insurance against a dying relationship. Neglect kills. It kills children, animals, plants, even machinery – and it kills marriages.

DIY *Beware of neglect! Ask each other: What kind of 'top-up' do we need?*
Eg. A coffee and chat weekly/daily?
A meal out together monthly?
One early bed and cuddle weekly?
A special celebration for our anniversary?
An away-break on our own?
A catch-up in the evenings after work?
An unexpected gift.
A fun time to look forward to, eg. a film?
Do we need to carry out any running repairs?

A Friend is...

A friend is someone who likes you.

A friend is someone who is truly interested in you and really cares.

If you need him or her, they'll be there, even if it costs them a lot.

A friend is someone with whom you dare to be yourself.

A friend is someone you can trust and feel safe with. You don't have to pretend.

With a friend you can breathe freely, you can say what you like, and even silence is comfortable.

A friend understands you, accepts your oddities and weaknesses, and goes on liking you.

You can laugh and cry together.

A friend is someone you like to be with, and to do things with.

Someone with whom you share common interests: sports, hobbies, films, music, travel, gardens, humour, social life.

Friendship is a priceless gift. Treasure it.

Used with permission.

'A Hug a Day Keeps the Blues Away'

'*C*onsider the hug. It is the perfect gift. One size fits all, and nobody minds if you exchange it.

'I've been given a rise!' he said as he came in from work. 'And I've booked us all a holiday in France on the strength of it!'

With half a skip she was flinging her arms round his neck. 'You're brilliant!' she grinned. 'How wonderful!'

He wrapped his long arms around her back and almost lifted her off the floor as he squeezed her tight. They laughed as they hugged.

She was about to go on night duty at the hospital. It had been a busy day with very little chance to sleep.

'I'd give anything to stay home tonight,' she said wearily.

He drew her close and held her face gently in his hands.

'I know,' he said, kissing her gently. Then he folded her into his arms and let her head rest on his shoulder while he stroked her hair.

'Let's hope it's an uneventful night tonight,' he said quietly, 'and the weekend's coming soon.'

She lifted her head and smiled. 'I must go,' she said, 'or I'll be late.' A final squeeze of the hand, then she grabbed her bag and was gone.

She was watching a robin in the garden when he looked out of the window and noticed her, her tousled brown curls, that little turned-up nose that he'd always loved. There was an interested, enquiring look on her face as she watched the robin perched on the fence post.

He opened the French window and, without a word, quietly walked up to her and hugged her.

'You're terrific,' he said. 'I could eat you for tea!' And he nibbled her ear playfully. She smiled so happily, and then joked, 'But you wouldn't get any more chocolate cakes if you did that!'

'You're better than a hundred chocolate cakes!' he said.

They came home from the hospital together. Her mother had been semi-conscious for three days, but today she'd lapsed into a coma, and it was only a matter of hours, they told her.

The babysitter tactfully stayed in the kitchen when they came in, to give them space. He shut the door and turned to her. She clung to him and sobbed, while he held her and stroked her back and shoulders, offering her a big handkerchief to mop up the tears.

'I can't believe she's going,' she wept. 'She's always been there. Oh Mum...' and she broke down again. He let her cry, till finally she took a deep breath and blew her nose loudly.

'I'll make you a cup of tea,' he said, and went to the kitchen.

She was on her own in the house when there was a knock at the door. She'd locked it, so she peeped out of a bedroom window to see who it was. A man stood there, his hat pulled well down so that she couldn't see his face. He wore dark trousers and a three-quarter-length black waxed coat. He carried no attache case or papers.

He knocked again, more loudly, and looked up at the windows, making her back away to avoid being seen. She caught a quick glimpse of a sharp nose and sallow complexion. Her heart began to race and her tummy turned over as fear gripped her. He tried the door knob, then walked round the side of the house, looking in at the windows. She determined not to let on that anyone was in, and eventually he walked back down the path, got into a black car, slammed the door and drove off.

She grabbed the phone. 'Gerry, there's been a man snooping round,' she told her husband. 'I'm scared.'

Gerry dashed home in his lunch hour and found Pam sitting in the kitchen, shaking like a leaf and clutching an undrunk cup of tepid tea in both hands.

She was so relieved and grateful to see him that she jumped up, spilling tea on the work top. He folded his arms round her and held her for what seemed like minutes till the shaking began to subside.

'I'm dead scared,' she whispered, 'but it's much better now you're here.'

'A hug makes you feel good all day.'

Hugs are a universal language. Couples can 'say it' with hugs, anywhere, anytime. No special setting is needed. A hug can be given and received whatever the weather or the time of day.

It makes happy days happier.

It makes impossible days possible.

Its benefits last long after it's over.

Hugs can be short or long – squeezy or gentle – friendly, joyful or tender.

This kind of hug, even between partners, has nothing to do with sex. It is quite distinct from a lover's embrace. It can be affectionate, playful, supportive, compassionate.

Hugs say it all – without words. Their value is greater than gold, a currency beyond price. They're worth more than a thousand words or even a thousand pounds. They give us encouragement and reassurance, and can be deeply satisfying.

Hugs must be offered sensitively. Not everyone is ready for a hug. For some, a pat on the shoulder, a squeeze of the hand or arm, may be the kind of touch they need. A thoughtless, unwelcome hug is an assault. A sensitive hug is a real gift.

If you were hugged as a child, you probably find it quite easy to hug your partner and your children. But not everyone is so fortunate.

Alan and Liz had been married for nearly forty years, but in all that time they had never had a hug. Liz couldn't hug anyone, not even her three sons or her grandchildren, although she longed to, and she didn't understand why. Then an opportunity came to talk to a counsellor, who helped her to realise afresh that her childhood had been very tough, and was a major contributing factor in her present problems. Her parents had hated each other and had no time or affection for Liz either. She felt isolated, as if she didn't belong to anyone or matter to anyone in the world. She tried to run away, but her mother's cutting remark: 'Nobody would want you' was enough to stifle even that desperate hope.

When she was able to realise that she was a person in her own right, of infinite value and importance, she gradually managed to leave the pain of the past behind. In the end, she was able to forgive her parents, who had

Hugs are...

Hugs comfort and heal.

Hugs release our feelings.

Hugs overcome fears.

Hugs dispel loneliness.

Hugs ease tension.

Hugs can say:

'You're special.'

'I love you.'

'I'm scared. I need you.'

'I want to share your pain.'

'I'm your friend. You can count on me.'

'I'm so glad you're here.'

'It's good to see you.'

'I forgive you.'

'Thank you.'

From *The little Book of Hugs* by Kathleen Keating.
Used with the permission of Harper Collins (Australia).

died years ago, for the things that happened to her in childhood, and healing began. Now Liz can hug her husband and her sons and grandchildren without qualms, and their family life has benefited enormously.

How can we rediscover the practice of hugging? 'A hug a day keeps the blues away.' Not a peck on the cheek or a hasty 'hello', but a proper hug.

One partner can gently coach the other, first with touch, then closer touch, then a little, quick hug, till he or she graduates to the real thing!

In the hurry and bustle of our daily lives, hugs happen all too rarely. Yet it only takes thirty seconds to have a good hug. Is thirty seconds really going to wreck our schedule for the day? On the contrary, the joy of the hug may spin us on our way with a lighter step.

If your wife is wearily plodding round the kitchen, trying to get a meal together after a hard day, why not gather her into your arms for a thirty seconder, then lay the table or peel the potatoes?

If your husband staggers through the door with a glazed look of exhaustion or depression, why not wrap your arms round his neck or back and hug him tight? It'll do him more good than a stiff drink!

N.B. Respond to the offer of a hug, even if you're in the middle of loading the washing machine or unpacking the weekly shop! Nothing is more hurtful than having your hug rejected.

A couple were having a meal, and she made a rather whimsical remark. He got up to kiss her, but in the middle of the kiss she complained that he'd hurt her ear by pressing against her earstud. A look of acute pain crossed his face. He didn't try again. One rejection was enough.

DIY

Hug each other lots.
If you can't hug very well yet, begin with
affectionate touch. As you feel safer, you'll learn
to hug.

If hugging is impossible for you, don't despair. Seek help. Like Liz, you will be able to find healing, and then the hugs will come.

Some ideas for this chapter come from 'The Little Book of Hugs' by Kathleen Keating, published by Angus and Robertson.

'You Look Wonderful Tonight!'

The following notice appeared in a newspaper:

'Best wishes on your birthday. Love from your friend, lover, chef, laundress, nurse, cleaner, banker, seamstress, gardener, entertainer, social secretary, poet, typist, apprentice, actor, telephonist, book-keeper, business partner, company secretary, writer, auditor, chauffer, slave-driver, confidante, hostess, debtor, personnel officer and wife – Kate.'

Incredible people, wives! Husbands, please note, and pass on some compliments. Wives, please note, husbands like compliments too.

It has been said that 'the only compliment some husbands pay their wives is to marry them'. How many compliments have you paid to your partner this week? It's not that we want to flatter each other, but we all need encouragement, whether we are at work or at home.

'You look great today.'

'This cake is delicious.'

'I was so proud of you at the meeting.'

'The book-ends you made are just right.'

'How lovely to come home to a tidy house tonight.'

'I can't see a single weed left in the garden. Thank you.'

'The car looks like new!'

'Thank you for doing the ironing.'

'It was such a help when you picked up my mum.'

'I really appreciate it when you wash up.'

'Thank you for arranging such a lovely outing.'

'You give the children so much time. They do love it.'

'It's a miracle the way you keep up with the washing for us all.'

'You've got such a great sense of humour. I love it.'

'How do you manage to be nice all day after so many broken nights? You're amazing.'

'You're the best cook for miles.'

'The children are always bathed and cheerful when I get home. You're one in a million.'

'I like the way you've had your hair cut.'

Giving encouragement, speaking words of appreciation, is like throwing logs on a fire. The embers burst into new flame and crackle with life.

One of the greatest compliments we can pay is to take a genuine interest in our partner's work, or the way their day has gone. Five or ten minutes of real listening gives the other a great sense of being valued.

Let's make a special effort too, to compliment our partner on things that mean a lot to him or her, but don't particularly interest us.

Eg. Get out into the garden and notice how well the roses are doing and how neat the edges are, even if you're not a gardener yourself.

Eg. Compliment your partner on the way they've organised a party for needy children.

Eg. Admire the sweater that's taken weeks to make, or the art work for a local event.

Saying something appreciative or kind about *anything* is always going to be a pleasure and give pleasure.

Warning. Critical remarks and negatives are like throwing a bucket of cold water on the fire. It takes at least four positive comments to wipe out one negative. Let's be very sparing with our buckets of water, and generous with logs.

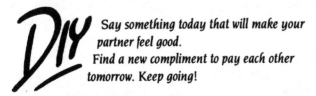

Say something today that will make your partner feel good.
Find a new compliment to pay each other tomorrow. Keep going!

Keep the Home Fires Burning

*D*inner for two by candlelight to the sound of soft music. Walking hand in hand along a palm-lined beach in the moonlight. Sitting close together on a hillside, watching the sunset on a warm summer evening.

What spells romance for you? We may not often be able to experience the kind of romantic dreams pictured here, but in reality, romance is wider than moonlight and candles, lovely as these can be. Romance is demonstrating our love for each other through words, attitudes and actions, in a myriad different ways, day by day.

Ray and Gill have been married for over thirty years. they have a teddy bear that lives in the bedroom, and if one of them has to be away for the night, the bear often tucks up on the other's pillow to await them at bed-time, sometimes with a little love-note held in his paws.

If one comes in late from a meeting and the other has gone to bed, the bear may be holding the toothbrush, hiding in the pyjamas or peeping out of a drawer. A tiny action, yet it says, 'Welcome home. I love you.'

The husband of a newly-married couple decided to make use of Valentine's Day to show his wife how special she was. He booked a table for two in a secluded restaurant, bought a rose, presented it to her and invited her out to dinner. She felt a million dollars! Romance can fit in with our particular interests and shared capacities.

A young man decided to propose to his girlfriend. They were both keen mountain climbers, so he drove her to the far North of Scotland, to the area of a high mountain named Ben Hope. Hidden in his rucksack he carried a half-bottle of champagne, two glasses, a ring and a camera.

They climbed to the summit, where a blizzard was raging. Undaunted, he knelt in the snow and proposed. He was accepted, they hugged, he burrowed in his rucksack for the ring and slipped it onto her half-frozen finger, they drank the hastiest of toasts – and recorded the moment on camera! Then two very happy people descended at high speed to the lower slopes of the mountain. Ben Hope had lived up to its name, and the next day they climbed the other 3,000-foot mountain in the area, Ben Loyal, in glorious sunshine!

This wouldn't be every couple's idea of the perfect engagement setting, but for them it was ideal. Romance must suit your taste or it won't be romantic!

A missionary couple with four children under six and a noisy little dog, once said, 'You have to work at staying sweethearts!' That may sound a contradiction in terms, but it's not. Once a year, on their wedding anniversary, those two somehow managed to get a babysitter willing to handle four children and a dog, and go out together for a meal. It couldn't be expensive – they didn't have much cash. But for them, it was a high priority.

The same husband, whenever he came home from a

working trip, tried to bring his wife a small bottle of toilet water from the duty-free, because to him, and to her, perfume was a special delight. She, for her part, would do her very best to wear good colours, do her hair (when he was out!) and take trouble with her make-up. She also kept a trim figure, which was an important part of how she felt about herself. She didn't feel desirable when she was overweight. The romance of this marriage has stood the test of time. It has flourished because both partners worked at it.

Surprises are another good way of saying 'I love you'

Have you seen an old black-and-white film recently? Aren't they dull when you're used to full colour? A marriage laundered of romance is a bit like the old black-and-white movie. It lacks variety, spice, colour, excitement, emotion.

So how do we re-kindle romance? Have you noticed any newly-wed couples lately? What made you think they were newly-weds? Unlike other travellers, reading newspapers, thumbing through the in-flight magazine, snoozing or just looking bored, the newly-weds probably sat close together, holding hands or surreptitiously stroking each other, and gazing into each other's eyes. May be they gently rubbed noses, laughed a little and kissed.

When did you last gaze into your partner's eyes? You may well find there the tenderness, the intimacy, the light, the sparkle and the gentleness that was there when you first met. The eyes don't change, and even if you don't readily have eye contact at the moment, it is surprising what a truly loving look can do. Your eyes can say, 'I love you' so clearly that the message can't be missed – only choose your time! It's no good if your partner has just messed up the fax machine or spilt coffee on the carpet.

Touch can say so much too. A hand resting on the shoulder, a soft brush of the cheek, a squeeze of the arm, a gentle stroke of the hair, a hand on the other's knee when sitting together, the meeting of feet under the table, a kiss on the back of the neck. We need to touch each other lovingly, not always sexually, for as we touch we're saying in an intimate, secret way, 'I love you. You're special.'

Birthdays and anniversaries are a great time to stimulate romance, but wives must remember that few men keep a note of such dates. They need some broad hints for weeks beforehand. 'Just think! We'll be five in a month's time!' 'Do you realise, I'm going to be out of my twenties/thirties/forties next birthday?' 'We got married in daffodil time, didn't we? It must be the eighth anniversary this April!'

Some good promptings, and you may find yourselves enjoying fun celebrations of these special occasions. How much better than nursing a grievance because your husband didn't remember.

Memories are a lovely way to rekindle romance. Get out the photo albums of your wedding, honeymoon or a good holiday, and reminisce together.

On our thirtieth wedding anniversary, my husband and I booked into the same room of the same hotel where we'd spent the first night of our honeymoon. It was wonderful! Visiting old haunts where you've had happy times can be such a good experience.

Clothes help or hinder romance. There's nothing romantic about tatty old gear, day or night. Dressing up for an occasion, taking real trouble, makes you feel good, look good and appreciate each other afresh. The stunner you married is there again! As for night-time, patched pyjamas and dreary, wash-weary nighties are a real turn-off. How about a visit to your favourite department store for the latest word in feminine nightwear? It might prove a great investment!

Surprises are another good way of saying, without words, that you love your partner.

Andy came in one day with a big grin on his face, to find Barbara drying her hands on her apron, looking tired and fraught.

'Guess what?' he said. 'I'm taking you away for the weekend!'

'What? All of us?'

'No, no. Just you.'

'But what about the children?'

'Nan's coming to look after them.'

'And my meeting tomorrow?'

'I've told them you can't make it. I said it was my fault. They've found someone else to stand in for you.'

'And who's going to exercise the dogs, and feed the rabbits?'

'It's all organised, I promise. Now all you have to do is pack a case, and we'll be off in a couple of hours. Nan'll be here any minute, so she'll do bath-time tonight. The children are all excited. They're looking forward to it.'

Andy gently untied Barbara's apron and hung it up behind the kitchen door. He wrapped his arms round his bewildered wife and whispered in her ear, 'It's going to be just you and me, and it's going to be great.'

She hugged him back. 'Thank you,' she said blinking away a tear. 'I can't believe it's really happening yet.' But she went off upstairs to pack.

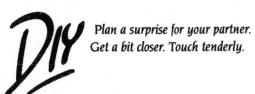

Plan a surprise for your partner. Get a bit closer. Touch tenderly.

We can't always make our surprises last a whole week-end, but 'un-birthday' presents that come out of the blue, a bunch of flowers, a box of chocolates or a phone call in the middle of the day just to say, 'I'm thinking of you' – every little surprise brings joy and pleasure, and feeds our love. Think what your partner would most appreciate. What new ways, or old ways since forgotten, can you think of that will say to him or her: 'You're special.' 'You're mine.' 'I love you.' 'This is our secret.'

'You have to work at staying sweethearts.' It doesn't

need to cost a lot of money, but it costs time and thought to nourish our romance and keep our relationship in full colour. And it pays a dividend way beyond our investment. We shall grow richer and richer in our relationship as the years go by if we go on investing in our marriage.

One Man's Meat...

Nigel and Sally were in love. Every spare moment they had they spent together: talking, walking, driving, eating, going to concerts, films, plays, opera. The more they saw of each other, the more they loved each other, until they announced to their not-at-all-surprised families that they were engaged.

Christmas came, and Sally found a large, exciting-looking parcel under the Christmas tree. What could it be? It was from Nigel, and she began to romanticise about the contents. A beautiful ornament perhaps? A smart shoulder bag? Some lovely shoes? A pretty lampshade?

Nigel presented it to her on Christmas Day, she opened it with great anticipation, the first Christmas present she had ever had from Nigel, and it was…a petrol can! A two-gallon petrol can, red and shiny, with a screw cap.

Sally was speechless. She didn't know whether to laugh or cry. Was it a joke?

'It looks like a petrol can!' she said, turning it over and over as if by magic it might suddenly become something else.

'It is! You've run out of petrol twice recently,' said Nigel, 'so I thought if you had this in the car, it would solve the problem.'

Nigel was being thoroughly practical. He couldn't

think of a more useful present. Sally felt completely let down. She was romantic and had hoped for a personal gift that would speak to her of Nigel's affection. It was their first lesson in being different.

Peter and Rosie sat down to plan a holiday. They agreed that all the family really needed a good break.

Peter began, 'Now let's think how much we can afford, once we've paid for...'.

'Oh no!' protested Rosie. 'Let's have a look at all those lovely brochures you picked up at the travel agent. Look! Here's a beautiful little hotel in the Tyrol, and a canal trip in France, and a special offer for four to Tunisia...'.

'Hang on a minute!' said Peter. 'First of all, let's look at dates and see when we're free to go away. We mustn't forget that Jamie's got Cub Camp and you've got that Summer School...'.

'But if we look in the brochures and find something lovely, we can see if the time fits afterwards.' Rosie began to dream: 'Think of lazy days by the sea, swimming whenever we feel like it, and sun-bathing to our hearts' content.'

It was hard for Peter and Rosie to plan anything, least of all a holiday. Peter wanted to look at all the practical details. Rosie just wanted to dream....

We're all so different from each other, aren't we? And it's all right to be the way we are, whether we're planners or dreamers, romantics or practical, football crazy or a nature-lover, good with our hands or good with our brain, reserved or extrovert, tidy or scatter-brained, lovers of food or lovers of ideas – whatever we're like, it's OK!

There's no 'right' and 'wrong' in our many personality differences. We've been built as unique individuals with our own particular blend of characteristics that make us who we are – and who we are is great! Not better, not inferior, but *me*, and OK.

While we're single we can indulge ourselves to some extent according to our likes and dislikes, but once we marry, we're into a completely new arena.

What about the people-loving woman, always inviting friends in, who marries a quiet, shy man who'd far rather have a peaceful evening alone with his wife?

What about the couple who win £300 in a competition and can't agree how to spend it? He wants to go and buy a new mower and some special tools. She wants to go off on a 'Take-a-Break' weekend.

How about the man who really enjoys cooking, but his wife refuses to have him in the kitchen because he uses all the butter and leaves the place looking as if a bomb's gone off?

How can we learn to live with our differences, yes, even to enjoy them, and certainly to laugh rather than cry over them?

The big word is COMMUNICATION. We have to *talk* about our differences. We need to make up our minds, in the early days, that whenever a problem like this crops up, we will discuss it – if not at once, then at an agreed time later. Then we'll begin to learn the art of compromise, of agreeing on a plan that we can both at least tolerate, and better still, come to enjoy!

Take the hospitality couple. They might agree to have people in once a week, or once a month.

The couple who won £300 might spend £150 on tools and £150 on a break-away night together.

The keen cook husband might have the run of the kitchen once, twice, three times a week, provided he clears up, and buys more butter if he uses it all, or at least writes it on the shopping list!

If we were all the same, think how dull life would be. How dreary our marriage might become without the stimulus of our differences. My husband has a wonderful sense of humour, and a great capacity to cheer people up and make them laugh. I'd be deadly without his sense of fun. He has a diary, and once something is entered there, it's more or less immovable. I much prefer to have spaces in mine, and leave duties like shopping, hairwashing or special cooking to fit in when they do. He writes notes all over the house – there are pads and pencils in nearly every room. This is highly efficient, but daunting too, because I don't write so many notes and I do forget. I leave things around the house. It looks 'homely', I think. He likes to tidy everything away – and then I can't find what I'm looking for!

I'm sure you could make a metre-long list of the differences between you and your partner. The great thing is to realise that no one's 'better' or 'worse' just because they do write notes or they don't like parties. It's not for any of us to make judgements about our partner because they don't tick the way we do.

We have embarked on a voyage of discovery – the discovery of a whole personality that is very different from our own. Sometimes the voyage is bewildering. Sometimes it's infuriating, sometimes fascinating. But it's never dull.

We have also embarked on a challenge – the challenge of working out ways to accommodate both our personalities without squashing either of them. The challenge of unselfishly blending our ways and desires so that we both feel happy and comfortable.

When Peter and Rosie finally decided on a holiday by the sea, their problems weren't over. They woke up the first morning to a glorious sunny day. Rosie lay back on the pillow and thought, 'What bliss! All day to do nothing! Swim, lie in the sun, eat a bit, swim, snooze…'.

'What are we going to do today?' Peter's question crashed through her reverie.

'Do? What d'you mean, do? We're on holiday! We don't have to do anything.'

'But we can't just lie on the beach all day and do nothing!'

'Why ever not? I don't want to move further than those waves all day.'

'But after you've had a swim, we can go to a chateau, or find an interesting little village or something…'.

In the end, they found a compromise. Beach all morning. Expedition in the afternoon. Now they've decided, a few years and holidays later, that a whole day of rest followed by a whole day of 'doing' is more fun, and they each actually enjoy the other's kind of day.

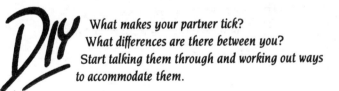

What makes your partner tick?
What differences are there between you?
Start talking them through and working out ways
to accommodate them.

The FURY Factor

What are the flash points in your partnership?

- ☐ Hogging the telephone.
- ☐ Garlic in the food!
- ☐ Squeezing the toothpaste tube in the middle.
- ☐ Snoring.
- ☐ Your partner's always late – or too early.
- ☐ Bagging the car.
- ☐ Dirty coffee cups all over the living room.
- ☐ No clean shirt on Monday morning.
- ☐ Not coming for meals when they're ready.
- ☐ Map-reading on a journey.
- ☐ Wanting to watch different TV programmes.
- ☐ Over-tidiness – so you can never find anything.
- ☐ Bringing people home without warning.
- ☐ Garden tools left dirty or in the garden.
- ☐ Muddy boots on the clean floor.
- ☐ Leaving the newspaper as if hit by a gale.
- ☐ Any other ideas?!

Talk with your partner about other flash points in your relationship. Write them down.

- ■ _____
- ■ _____
- ■ _____
- ■ _____

How many of these things make you boil inside? Be honest! But remember that you are responsible for your own feelings. It's no good blaming your partner for the way you feel. We come face to face with ourselves in the closeness of a relationship, and we don't always like what we find – so we blame each other.

'You're never ready on time.'

'It drives me wild the way you…'.

Every couple has fury factors. How should we handle them?

The only way that works is to talk about them when they are not happening, and work out ways of dealing with them.

If one leaves the paper in a mess, he or she must either learn to tidy it or buy another one.

If one tidies everything away in unfindable places, he or she will have to find it.

If one squeezes the toothpaste tube in the middle and the other prefers to roll it up from the bottom, have a tube each. It's no more expensive in the end.

If one can't read a map or tell right from left, let the other do the map-reading while the first drives.

If you can't agree on the same programme, take it in turns to have the one you like.

Whatever the flash point, there has to be a solution, and we have to find it or we shall have an explosion on our hands. We can't afford to let things boil inside. When they boil over, someone's going to get hurt, and that someone is probably our partner.

Weathering Stormy Seas

Tony came in and heaved a large package onto the kitchen table, a look of slightly smug pleasure on his face.

'What have you got there?' asked Caroline.

'Oh, just a few tools,' Tony answered, trying to sound as casual as he could.

'More tools!' Caroline responded angrily. 'And how much did *they* cost?' Sheepishly, Tony pulled the invoice out of his pocket – £139.50.

'Almost £140! How *could* you?' yelled Caroline. 'Our credit cards are almost over the limit and both the girls need new shoes. The fridge is dying, and you know I'm only on part-time work.'

'But there was a sale on, and if I'm going to do a good job, I need good tools.'

'Not *now*,' Caroline was half furious and half in tears. 'I can't possibly get the girls any shoes now, and you know how bad it is for their feet to wear tight ones. You're *always* buying things you don't really need. You didn't ask me if we needed anything urgently. Suppose the fridge gives up? What then?'

'But I *do* need the tools. And I saved 10% on two of them! Why are you always angry when I buy something instead of enjoying it with me?'

'Enjoying it!' Caroline spat the words out and stamped her foot so hard that it hurt. She ran out of the kitchen, banging the door loudly.

Is conflict inevitable? Does every couple have rows? Or is there something wrong with us?

No, there's nothing 'wrong' with couples who have arguments. It could even be that the couples who never argue are the ones who are 'odd'. After all, we're all human, so from time to time we are going to clash, especially with the one who lives closest to us. In fact, the closer we are, the greater the chance of conflict, and sadly, the greater the chance of hurt and pain too.

Why do these quarrels begin? Where are we coming from?

When we marry, we bring a whole trunk full of baggage with us from our life until that moment. There may be family rows in there, a frightening experience or two, some painful rejections, past relationships that have left scars, and a whole host of other things that are attached to each of us. It's only a matter of time before these unwelcome experiences rear their heads in our marriage and threaten to cause trouble.

Derek and June were just about to get into bed on their first night home from honeymoon. He began to open a window and pull back the curtains. She sat bolt upright in bed and shouted, 'No! Don't open the window. I can't stand having the window open!'

'But it's warm tonight and there's not much traffic.'

'I don't care. I'm not having the window open!'

'But I *always* sleep with the window open. I'll wake up with a splitting headache if it's shut all night.'

'All right. Have it your own way. I'll go and sleep on the floor next door.'

June got out of bed and headed for the door, but Derek stopped her with his arm and drew her to him kindly.

'Come back to bed and let's talk about it.'

Reluctantly, she joined him in bed and he asked her gently, 'Is there some special reason why you don't like the window open?'

His tenderness melted her and she cuddled up to him.

'It makes me scared,' she confided. 'Once, when I was in bed at home, a man climbed up and started to get in through the window. I screamed and Dad came and the man ran off, but I've never opened the window at night since.'

They had a hug, and Derek pointed out to her that now, instead of Dad in another room, she had a husband right beside her – and anyway, the small town where they were now living was completely different from the rough area of her childhood. After talking it through, June felt reassured and Derek understood, and they agreed on a *little* bit of window. Gradually, as her confidence grew, they opened it more, and so the problem was solved.

By inspecting the baggage, Derek and June discovered what had triggered their argument, and were able to sort it out. Sometimes it's just family habits that cause problems.

Ed's mum had always done his washing and ironing, made his bed, cooked and washed up. In fact, she'd done everything for him.

Maureen's parents both worked, shared the chores, and expected the children to clean their own rooms, help with washing up, do their washing and ironing, and cook the evening meal once a week.

In the first few weeks of marriage, Ed tended to sit back and expect Maureen to run round after him, although she too had a full-time job. But Maureen wasn't going to let him get away with it.

'Ed, you can jolly well help me do the dishes instead of just switching on the telly.'

'Why should I?'

'Why should you? Why *shouldn't* you? I've been working just as long hours as you. Do you think it's fair to expect me to come home and do all the jobs here too?'

Reluctantly, Ed got out of his armchair, switched off the TV and slowly approached the sink.

'I'll wash, you dry,' said Maureen briskly, and she began to pile up wet plates. Ed took ages to dry each one, but she was totally unsympathetic.

'You'll get quicker with practice,' she said with studied cheerfulness, and left him to it while she made coffee.

It was the same with the vacuuming, dusting and emptying the rubbish bin.

'But that's your job, not mine!' he would protest.

'Well, it may have been in your home but it wasn't in mine. Dad helped Mum a lot and it's only fair to share the home jobs if we both work.'

For a while, Ed hated it, but he also had to agree that it was only fair. As he learned to do simple jobs around the house, he began to find them quite satisfying, and now, five years on, he and Maureen make a good partnership. But they wouldn't live through that first year again for anything!

Sometimes, it's differences in our personalities that cause conflict.

Patrick and Clare set off with the children to get some new school uniform and have lunch at McDonald's. On the way to Brighton, Clare saw a notice saying: 'Country Fayre'.

'Oh look!' she said. 'There's a Country Fayre at Falmer today and it's a sunny day. Let's go and see what it's like.'

'But we're going to buy the children's uniform,' Patrick protested. 'We can't go to the Fayre.'

'Why not? It might be raining another day, and besides, it's ages since we all did something fun together.'

'Yes, please, Dad!' chorused the children. 'Let's go to the Fayre! Shopping's *boring!*'

Patrick was thoroughly put out by this time.

'We came to get that uniform, and we're going to get that uniform, Fayre or no Fayre.' And he drove past the turning and down into the town with three extremely cross people in the car.

Patrick and Clare are so different. Patrick is an organised person with a Filofax full of appointments that he keeps to the minute. He does not like changes of plan! Clare, on the other hand, is a spontaneous person, flexible and not too bothered about the time. That's just the way they are, and both kinds of person are equally valid and important. There's nothing wrong with being flexible and nothing super right about keeping a list of appointments and living by the clock. But it doesn't always feel that way. How often we wish our partner was more like ourselves!

'If only he would stop looking at his watch and just enjoy what we're doing…'.

'If only she'd stop rushing off on crazy schemes when we've agreed to do something definite…'.

DIY Pinpoint one or two areas where your expectations differ.
Eg. Jobs around the home.
The importance of sticking to plans.
Try to work out compromises that you can both live with.

Letting Go

O nce, discussing his divorce with me, a friend of mine said, 'I had a terrible feeling of failure. Even though I felt that the divorce had been "right" and was "not my fault", I still felt that after many years as a married man, I had failed. I had become a national statistic.

'I'll never forget the court that day. I waited outside with about twenty other failures. We went in. The judge sat beneath the coat of arms. He read out all our names. Then he pronounced our marriages dissolved. It took twenty seconds to turn twenty-nine years into nothing. It was awesome and humiliating. It took me many years to get over that feeling of failure. And my fear was: "I've failed once. Will I fail again?"'

Less than 30% of second marriages, and less than 15% of third marriages, survive five years. The odds are not in our favour. Yet thousands of couples start out again hopefully every year, little realising, when they fall in love, the obstacles they will have to overcome. If they are divorced, the agony and sense of failure and remorse has to be reckoned with. If either has been widowed, the dead partner inevitably lives on in memory, able to cause painful and anxious comparisons with the present partner. If one has been single, their very independence, and lack of experience of marriage and divorce, can put a great gulf between the new couple, creating barriers that have to be painstakingly broken down.

Like an icy mountain full of slippery rocks and treacherous ledges, the new marriage presents the climbers with a huge challenge. They need to be sure they want to set out on the climb. They need specialist equipment in terms of forgiveness, patience and love to overcome the dangers, and, above all, an absolute determination to reach the top.

Dick and Marianne had just married and moved into Dick's home – a great mistake, they soon discovered. 'New marriage, new home,' they advised friends later. It was the second marriage for both of them, but neither of them had children.

Marianne admitted, 'I just can't get rid of her. I open the cupboards and there *she* is: the jam-pot that got pushed to the back when Dick was living alone – did she put it there? And every night I sit in our bedroom at the dressing-table I know *she* sat there and Dick watched her from the bed. Did he read all the time as he does with me? Or did he watch her and adore her curves?'

It's desperately hard not to worry about the ex-partner. The comparisons are endless. The two new partners need to express their love and appreciation of each other even more than in a first marriage, until it's possible to rest in confidence that each is the very best for the other.

Dick and Marianne had been very cautious when they first met. They had both been badly hurt by their previous marriage and divorce, and didn't want to get hurt again. They were careful to talk through their past experiences.

They both realised how important it was to get to know each other really well before making any decisions. They knew that depth was more important than the thrills of romance.

One day, they made a great mistake. They revisited an old haunt where Dick and his ex-wife had often spent the weekend.

Dick said, 'As I drove down the road towards the village I knew that we should never have gone. There it was – the pub we were to have lunch in. Why did we come? As we went in I recognised the place and back it all came. Marianne seemed happy, but all I could sense was the ghost of Jan at the bar, and the stairs that led up to the first floor where our bedroom had been. Ugh. I'll never do that again. Jan and I had a blazing row that weekend, anyway. In future I'll keep well out of the past. Never go back.'

Moving straight from one relationship into another is almost guaranteed to bring problems. The break-up of a marriage is full of pain – a far cry from the easy experience usually presented by the media. Both parties are inevitably left feeling bruised and battered, and quite possibly angry, bitter, resentful and a failure.

It takes time to work through these feelings. Somehow, we shall have to forgive and let go of the first marriage partner, if we are going to make it the second time round. It isn't easy, but it's essential, otherwise we'll bring the bad feelings into the new relationship, and all the old problems will start again.

It helps to tie up as many loose ends as possible from the first marriage before going ahead with the second: the sale of the home, financial arrangements, property, and resettling the children. These plans need to be in place, otherwise we're storing up trouble for the future.

If either party has been widowed or divorced, it is important to make sure that they have fully recovered before a new friendship develops. Until then, they are not ready for a new relationship. How easy it is to fall in love with the first person who shows genuine sympathy, but a lasting marriage cannot be built on sympathy. It has to be based on shared hearts and minds and close friendship.

Oliver and Meg had some of their biggest struggles over past friends. They often felt cut out when friends shared memories of which one of them was not a part, or laughed over old jokes, or reminisced over holidays and brought out photographs.

Meg felt that Oliver's friends were sizing her up, judging her against his former wife, and she hated it. Then they were both invited to the wedding of one of Meg's friends. It was terrible! Oliver knew no one and was bored stiff. Meg couldn't enjoy it because she was so aware of how he was feeling. When they got home, they poured themselves a drink and sat down.

'Don't let's *ever* go to a wedding again,' said Oliver.

'It was horrible,' agreed Meg, 'but what shall we do if a really good friend invites us?'

'Just say we can't make it. All those people I'd never seen before – and all your friends looking me up and down.'

'I thought you did really well,' said Meg. 'They all thought you were great.'

'And a big white cake, and speeches and all that. It brings back such painful memories.'

Even plain, harmless furniture can spark off a bitter argument.

Paddy and Susan came from very different first marriages. Paddy was self-employed, earning a moderate salary, while Susan had been married to a well-off business man and was used to a wealthier lifestyle.

He thought many of her belongings were flashy and unhomely, while she thought his were shabby and dull. Slowly, very slowly, they learned to accept each other's things and live with (most) of them, but it took a long time and caused many arguments.

Second marriages *can* work. Many do. But no one who has attempted it is going to pretend that it's like a Sunday afternoon stroll. It's a long haul, and only the really determined are going to get there.

The key, as always, lies in good communication. We have to keep in close touch with each other. Whatever we can talk through, we can probably work through, and whatever we can work through, we can almost certainly live through. Don't give up! KEEP TALKING – and you can make it.

 Keep in close touch.
When you have a problem, talk about it.

Parents and Step-parents

A second marriage brings a whole new set of tough problems if there are children (of any age) from either or both previous marriages. Even if they are grown up and have left home, they can make or mar a second marriage.

They may be totally against the new marriage from the start, and do everything in their power, which is considerable, to wreck it. They may feel bitterly angry, rejected, betrayed, strangely guilty, wildly jealous, or a mixture of all these things. Because of this, they can be slightly difficult to handle or just plain impossible.

The damage done to children, the pain inflicted on them by the break-up of their family, is beyond description. However wisely and lovingly they are handled, facts are facts. Mum and Dad have split, and so has their world.

Then one parent falls in love. They smile, laugh, hold hands and are happy with this stranger who visits more and more...and the one person who was there to give security and comfort, seems less and less available. No wonder children don't like their parents to marry again.

Jim and Tina thought it was time they told the children about the future. Jim recalls the painful scene.

'I well remember the time when we both felt it was

right to tell Tina's two children that we were going to get married and that their mother was to have a new husband. We sat them down in the living room – Julie aged ten and David aged eight. We gently explained to them both that over the past year or two we had become fond of one another and loved each other. So we were going to get married and we would all live together and make a new family home together.

My future wife explained that she loved them very much and that this would make no difference to that relationship. She also explained that they would all have so much more fun because we could now do things together as a family. They listened while their eyes got bigger and bigger. Then, like a bomb exploding, the reaction came. Julie burst into tears, ran out of the room and flung herself onto her bed, while David stood up, gave me a withering glance and stormed out of the house, slamming the front door as he went. Tina and I looked at each other speechless. So, I thought, this isn't going to be easy.'

The challenge now becomes one of trying to weld two families together, not just two people. The children are there from the very beginning of the relationship, and can often see what's coming before their parents. They tend to be resentful of the newcomer, suspicious and sometimes hostile, especially if they have reached their teens or beyond. Their loyalty remains with the former parent. Any newcomer is viewed as an intruder.

The children have probably been living with one parent, and the longer this has been going on, the more the children feel they have a right to that parent's undivided love and attention. The single parent has also had to adjust to standing alone, with no mate to help. For both parent and children, the change is going to be extremely difficult.

Some time after the painful interview described by Jim above, he reflected:

'Perhaps if we'd been open with Tina's children from the start, and told them exactly what was going on, it wouldn't have been so bad.

'Two of my sons, who were in their twenties, flatly refused to attend our wedding. It took them six years to accept the situation, whereas the third one, who came, accepted it much more easily. Somehow, we should have persuaded the others to come. It would have helped them to accept the new state instead of running away from it. After ten years, it's still not easy.'

Jim did his utmost to build friendship with David, but it was hopeless. David seemed to hate him...until one day they went to Brands Hatch together to watch the motor racing. They were driving across the field to park their car when Jim, on a sudden impulse, put David in the driving seat. 'His face lit up. I showed him how to work the gears and the clutch and off we went. We jerked! We bounced! It didn't do the clutch much good – but it broke the ice between us, and from then on, we began to build. **Doing something together** had done the trick. For David, motor racing paled into insignificance!'

Jim made it with David, but sometimes the stepchild is impossible. If this does happen, we have to remember that our *first* priority is our marriage. The children will be gone in due course, but we have a lifetime to live together. No difficult child must be allowed to drive a wedge between us, try as he will. We must do our utmost to make friends with our stepchildren, but not at the expense of our marriage.

We also do well to remember that a new parent can never replace the former parent, unless perhaps the children are very small. It is better to try to create a special relationship as a friend.

Jon married a widow, and described his struggle to compete with his stepson's dead father.

'There it was. Every day I went into George's room it looked down at me. His father. Now dead. This huge photograph fixed to the wall and assessing me. Day after day, day after day. It began to haunt me. It began to live. Try as I might, I could not seem to erase the former father and take his place. When we moved house, and when George moved his room, the photo would go with him. His father, who died when George was one, was still the dominant figure in his life, and I could not get near. The photograph brooded over me and I found it impossible to compete. So I gave up. I stopped trying to replace his father. I just became a father figure.

'Years passed. And then, one Father's Day, George gave me a card which read: "To Jon...(Dad)", and I was through. I couldn't believe it; he loved me as a father.'

The dead parent was probably no saint, but we must always respect a child's memory of a parent who has died. The older the child, the more space they need for this. If it is workable, contact with the dead parent's family can be very healing and helpful. They may be aunts, uncles, grandparents and cousins who have a lot to contribute to the child as well.

Discipline is an area fraught with problems. Wherever possible, it is better for parents to discipline their own children. The children may angrily resent

Do's & Don'ts
for second marriages
— by one who has been there

1. **Do** learn to live independently before starting a new relationship.

2. **Do** try to recover from the grief or divorce before starting a new relationship.

3. **Don't** live together before marriage. Don't rush.

4. **Don't** live in the previous spouse's house. If you have to, be sensitive.

5. **Don't** dwell in the past. Live in the present. Look to the future.

6. **Do** put your spouse first. Treat children equally.

7. **Do** allow your spouse time with his/her own children. Let their own parent discipline them.

8. **Do** spend regular time alone together.

9. **Do** learn to laugh – and laugh again.

10. **Do** always communicate, communicate, communicate.

being disciplined by the new parent, and try to play one off against the other. Blood against blood. When the chips are down, 'my' children would never behave like that. 'Your' children are simply unbearable. We have to try to teach ourselves that all the children are now ours, and to deal with them fairly and equally. A child may try to have secrets with his/her parent, but this causes division between the new parents unless they share the secret together. This isn't easy, but it is essential if the children are to be truly our children.

Doug and May decided not to have a honeymoon because they thought it would upset the children too much. So they all went home together after the reception. The cat crossed the threshold first, then the children, then the bride! The children didn't have the double shock of 'losing' their own parent and then being parked with friends or an aunt while the couple disappeared on honeymoon.

The only trouble about this was that Doug and May had no opportunity to get to know each other as a married couple.

'We had no chance even to sit down and have a quiet cup of tea together. There was always *someone* around, even last thing at night.'

'And worse still,' May added, 'the children had been so used to wandering into my bedroom that they went on doing it. It was very hard to explain to them, without causing hurt and jealousy, that this was no longer on. We had some hairy moments before they got the message!'

Doug commented: 'We recommend everyone to have a honeymoon if it's at all possible. But remember to give the children the hotel telephone number, and remind them to use your new name when they ask for you.

There might be a few raised eyebrows when they ask for 'Mr Stanford' and 'Mrs Gardener'!

Children continue to need time with their own parent, but they also need to be involved in the new family as much as possible. Tell them when a pregnancy begins, and keep them up to date with progress. Ask for their ideas about family holidays. Seek their views on redecorating, or a new family car, or anything else that affects them. This will help them to feel part of the new family.

Invent traditions that are special to the new family, such as ways of celebrating Christmas and birthdays, or having family fun times at weekends. This gives the family a sense of identity. It helps children to feel that they're special, that this is their family, and that they belong.

Another couple mentioned the importance of trying to share hobbies and interests with their new family. This helps to build bridges. Plenty of spoken appreciation and praise will help the children's confidence to grow again. Children often feel rejected after a divorce, and they need lots of extra encouragement to restore their self-esteem.

In a second family, most major rows are likely to stem from the fact that two families are involved. Anyone who has tried to form a new music group or new sports team, knows how difficult it is to get a varied group of people to work and play well together.

Put them under one roof, make them share all their meals together, have one pot of money, one living room, one television, washing machine, bathroom and cooker, and it begins to resemble the situation in a new joint family.

Add to this mix the strong and severely damaged emotions of those involved, and a picture starts to emerge – rather like an abstract painting with objects at bizarre angles. Out of this medley, a blend has to be created if the new family is going to settle down and be happy.

It takes enormous care and understanding to achieve it, but despite the pitfalls, it can be done. Plenty of thoughtfulness, a positive attitude on both sides, and lots of humour works wonders.

Given love, unselfishness, patience and perseverance, the new family will gradually blend together to make a harmonious home. There are families to prove it. The miracle does happen. A new family can be born.

Go for it!
And don't take 'no' for an answer!

Love-making Is an Art

'*J*ust add boiling water and stir!' say the adverts for instant coffee, cup-a-soups and chocolate drinks. The expressions on the drinkers' faces imply total satisfaction and pleasure.

We live in an age when many have been led to believe that sex is as readily available and satisfying as a cup of coffee. 'Just have sex and hey presto – it'll be great!'

Nothing could be further from the truth, as many a disappointed honeymoon couple who have waited until marriage will testify. Early attempts at love-making are more likely to resemble the first go at planning a flower border, icing a birthday cake or entertaining the in-laws for the whole of Christmas.

Like every other art, love-making is a skill to be learned, and we learn as we practise, and as we share with each other what we really enjoy. All those glossy magazines and glamorous, sexy films would have us believe that sex is bliss for any couple who find each other attractive, but of course in films, no one ever feels tired, or has a headache, or has just had a frantic day looking after three small children or rushing round the office, school or clinic. In films, no one walks in at the crucial moment, the telephone never rings, there is always plenty of time, and the mutual pleasure of the occasion is taken for granted.

But life isn't like that, is it?

Before Robert and Heather got married, they had been to lots of films and read romantic novels, and they fully expected their honeymoon to be packed with exciting love-making.

Even though they had both had previous partners, they had waited until their marriage for love-making. The wedding night was not as they had hoped. Each was silently comparing the other to earlier experiences, and instead of the delightful novelty of exploring each other and sensitively reaching the moment of entry, they failed to satisfy each other, and fell asleep disappointed and miserable.

'I thought that was it,' said Heather. 'We just weren't going to have a good time sexually. So I became tense, and that upset Robert, and we never really gave it a chance. I didn't reach a climax, Robert felt he'd "failed", and it became an area of tension between us. Our honeymoon was a real flop.

'It wasn't till we read a good book on the subject that we realised how foolish we'd been. We hadn't *talked* together about it. We hadn't said how we felt or what we liked or didn't like. And we'd been far too serious. Once we learned to have a laugh, change positions and try again, it helped a lot. Now we chat a lot and treat the whole thing more light-heartedly – and it's great!'

A man and a woman are physically quite different from each other, and are designed to fit together literally as 'one body'. Sexual intercourse is intended to be the ulti-mate expression of two people's deep love for each other, and of their life-long commitment to one another. Their oneness is expressed in the merging of their bod-ies as they give themselves completely to each other. It is part of the awesome statement we make to each other in the wedding service: 'All that I have I give to you. All that I am I share with you.'

Sex was designed to be the celebration of a relationship, not the purpose of it. It was intended to be beautiful, pure and innocent, and to be within the context of marriage. It is the language of true, deep, committed love, the language of trust.

Sadly, we have moved a long way from that wonderful, original plan.

Penny put it this way. 'Mike comes in from work, grunts hello, helps himself to a drink, and crashes in front of the telly. He never asks me about my day, how I'm feeling or

how my job is going. I have to badger him even to go
and say goodnight to the children.

'Then he asks what's for supper, puts it on a tray, goes
off to his computer and starts typing. We hardly ever have
supper together, and he never says it tastes good. I go on
with the chores, because why sit down on my own?
When I feel tired, I go off to bed. Maybe I'll have a bath,
and half way through, Mike comes in. He sees me lying
there, and immediately bends down and starts fondling
me. Or if I'm in bed, he'll get undressed, climb in beside
me, and pull me towards him with obvious intent.

'I can't face it. He's ignored me all evening, hardly said
a word. Then he gets all sexed up and expects me to
respond. When I refuse, he gets angry or thinks he's "no
good in bed" or something. It's nothing to do with that. I
just can't suddenly make love when he's treated me all
evening as if I didn't exist.'

DIY Buy a good book on sex in marriage. (See
'More Ideas'.) Read it in bed together!
Remember that love-making is a skill to be
learned. Enjoy practising it.

It has been said that if a man wants a good half-hour,
he must watch the other twenty-three and a half! Men
and women are very different in this area. A man can
separate his day from his sex life, living a frenetic day
in the work place, and still finding reserves of energy
for making love. He can separate his relationship with
his wife from his sexual desires too, quarrelling with
her when he gets home, yet being quickly aroused by
the sight of her taking her clothes off or by a waft of

her talc or perfume. The fact that the quarrel hasn't been resolved may make no difference to him, whereas to his wife, it is central. She cannot bring herself to make love when the last words she exchanged with her husband were angry ones. To her, love-making is an inseparable part of their relationship, an expression of warmth and affection. If her man hasn't been loving and affectionate, she won't want sex. A woman's greatest sex organ is her heart.

As far as possible, the day should be a foretaste of the evening. A few extra kisses and snuggles and whispered 'I love yous' stir up desire. A gentle fondling in the kitchen, a special hug when we part in the morning, or an extra warm greeting on return from work, all help to prepare for a good time later. So does a meaningful compliment such as: 'You're delicious. Let's have a date tonight' or 'See you later, sweetheart.' Help with the dishes may stimulate companionship too.

Spoken words of appreciation, encouragement and affection also help to build our self-esteem and improve our sex life. If you don't put your thoughts into words, how can your partner know what you're thinking? A man who is frequently told: 'You're so wonderful / clever / good-looking / wise / such a super Dad'; a woman who is told: 'You look so pretty / you've done brilliantly / I love the way you laugh / walk / hold your head as you brush your hair' – are much more likely to respond to each other's sexual advances than a couple who hardly speak except about the garden, politics, the neighbours or football.

In other words, love-making is, in a sense, an all-day affair. The better we've related during the day, the better that last half-hour will be.

It's fun to go up to bed hand in hand or arm in arm.

Love making is a skill to be learned!

If you decide to have a bath, you may like to undress each other and get under the bubbles together for a bit of 'play-time' before getting into bed. By the time you are both lying down, your desire for each other will lead to further foreplay and your love-making will be a delight and joy for you both.

It may take a while for an inexperienced couple to learn to reach an orgasm together. Indeed some couples never manage it, but we can still have a thoroughly satisfying sex life. The husband can gently arouse his wife after his orgasm, and bring her to a climax before they both relax, holding each other closely as the wife slowly 'cools'. Remember that a man is quickly aroused and quickly 'dies down', rather like a gas cooker, whereas you could say a woman is more like an electric cooker, slow to warm up, staying 'hot' for longer, and cooling down slowly. She likes to be held and cuddled for a while after the excitement is over.

As we get to know each other and grow together in every way, so we shall develop our love-making into something we look forward to and thoroughly enjoy. The important thing to remember is that it is an integral part of our relationship, and will only thrive as the rest of our friendship and love thrives.

Perfecting the Art

or both partners to enjoy their love-making to the full, they need to do their best to meet each other's needs. Fulfilment comes from giving rather than getting. If we focus on how best to please our partner, we shall receive increasing pleasure ourselves as we succeed in giving it. If we're trying to please ourselves, we shall find less and less satisfaction. We can end up in a kind of mutual masturbation session rather than love-making.

Any normal man will reach a climax during intercourse, but for him to become a good lover is another story. Given a sheet of paper and some paints, anyone can produce a picture of sorts, but only the artist creates a thing of beauty. Even if he has a real gift, he still spends years learning and practising before he is able to paint pictures that both he and his customers will enjoy.

A loving husband will take time to discover what his wife really enjoys and finds stimulating. He will invite her to tell him what she most likes, or when she may be a bit sore or sensitive. They will talk as they make love, expressing their pleasure and excitement, getting the timing better so that the wife is really ready for her husband to come inside her, experimenting with different positions according to their mood or what they find excites them.

The wife need not be a passive partner, always waiting for her husband to take the initiative, but can set about arousing her husband if she is keen to make love. She will soon discover what does it. It may be a particular scent, or seductive nightwear – everyone is different, there is no 'right' or 'wrong' way to communicate with our partner. Music that has romantic associations may be just what's needed, or he may respond more to a long, mouth-to-mouth kiss, especially if her hands are wrapped round his neck or buried in his hair – if he still has some!

James and Joan had learned the art of pleasing each other fully. After a pleasant day off, they would have supper by the fire or in the kitchen, then read for a bit or listen to music.

James would suggest an early bed, which usually gave Joan a signal. They would go upstairs arm in arm, and James set the bath going, and began to undress Joan, kissing her neck and shoulders and stroking her as he did so.

Only one dim light shone in the bedroom, and after a lazy bath, they fondled each other as they dried, becoming increasingly aroused. James sometimes picked Joan up and carried her to bed, where their foreplay became more and more exciting, until the moment of total union came.

When the climax was over, they continued to lie together, holding each other close, until gently, sleepily, they drew apart and dozed off amid murmurs of pleasure. They were practised lovers, and their love-life had becoming fulfilling and extremely enjoyable for both of them – but it had taken a while to get there.

There's no way that a man can know by magic how to please his wife in bed, nor can a woman know what most pleases her husband unless he tells her. We need to talk about our love-making in order to discover what will give both of us the greatest excitement and pleasure. Doing a questionnaire together might be helpful.

'Variety is the spice of life.' It's the spice of love-making too. Why stick to bed-time? If you can be sure of privacy, why not enjoy the fun of making love in the middle of the day?

John had lost interest in sex. Work was so demanding, and kept him away from home for such long hours, that he came home exhausted. He was also discouraged because he wasn't being promoted. Others seemed to be doing so much better than he was. Julia was longing for him to make love to her, but she understood his problems, so she made up her mind to give him plenty of encouragement. She greeted him with real warmth when he came home from work, and gave him time to talk about the day and unwind. She made a point of noticing anything positive he said and congratulating him on it.

She also bought herself a pretty, lacy nightie and some eau de toilette that she knew he liked, and took care to look her best on Saturday and Sunday evenings when John wasn't quite so tired.

It worked. John began to regain self-esteem, and to notice her and feel drawn towards her. She responded warmly, and gradually their love-life was rekindled.

With Diana it was she who was too tired, but she and Keith invented a game.

'I'm going to lie here and pretend you don't exist, that I can't feel anything.' So she would see how long she could lie completely still, while Keith fondled various parts of her body. It was never very long before her tiredness disappeared and she became thoroughly keen.

Every couple will find their own level of frequency, and this may well change with the circumstances of life. For some, three times a week is normal. For others, once a week or once a month suits them fine. Some often cuddle and kiss but less often have intercourse. Others can't possibly stop till they get there!

A man, especially a younger man, is very often keener to have intercourse than a woman, and here again, we have the opportunity to give to one another. A husband shouldn't be too demanding, but nor should his wife refuse him often, even if she doesn't at first feel inclined.

A pregnant wife or the mother of a young baby becomes very absorbed with the child and can lose all interest in sex. This is a real danger zone, and it is most important for the husband to be sensitive, and also for the wife to sacrifice her own desire sometimes to satisfy her husband's. He cannot be expected to last too long without sex, and may be tempted to go and find it elsewhere if he gets desperate. Amid the nappies and the bottles, a wife somehow needs to be a lover too, and she will in fact enjoy it enormously once she switches her mind onto the idea. The mind is a powerful sex stimulus.

Sex is not the measure of our love. A recent survey of 90,000 women found that 70% wouldn't mind if they never had sex again, so long as they were held closely and tenderly. Our love for each other can be expressed in a hundred different ways, and sex is only one of them.

If a husband recognises that his wife is simply too tired for sex, perhaps there are jobs around the house that he can do for the time being at least, while the baby is small, that will relieve her, and so help her to rest a bit and feel more inclined to make love. He will be benefiting himself, and helping their marriage to deepen too, as they share this new stage in their life together.

All this talk of sex may make some couples feel there must be something wrong with them if they don't make love very often. Not at all. We are all different, and as long as we're both happy with our situation, that's fine. If one of us is not satisfied, then we need to talk about it, and the sooner the better. This kind of frustration quickly builds up, which is the last thing we want.

Nevertheless, as we talk about it together, keep our sense of humour, experiment with various positions, places and times, and show mutual respect, our love-making will become an increasingly pleasurable part of our relationship. The more we give, the more we'll receive.

What are your views on the following statements?

		Yes	No
1.	It's the woman's job to use a contraceptive.	☐	☐
2.	Sex is for the bedroom only.	☐	☐
3.	It should happen daily/weekly/monthly.	☐	☐
4.	The man should always initiate sex.	☐	☐
5.	An orgasm is not essential on every occasion.	☐	☐
6.	Sexual intercourse is the only way of expressing intimacy in a marriage.	☐	☐
7.	Personal cleanliness is important.	☐	☐
8.	Tenderness is more important than technique.	☐	☐
9.	One partner should never deny the other.	☐	☐
10.	Within marriage, anything goes sexually.	☐	☐
11.	A good book on sex in marriage can be helpful.	☐	☐
12.	It is important to discuss our sex life together.	☐	☐
13.	Different times and varying positions are a good idea.	☐	☐
14.	Can we think of ways to improve our love-making?	☐	☐

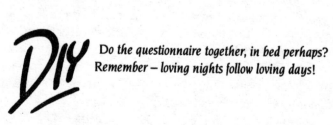

Do the questionnaire together, in bed perhaps?
Remember – loving nights follow loving days!

Watch Out...There's a Thief About!

'The chemistry was so strong, I just couldn't resist. He was the first person to make me feel really special.'

'I didn't think it'd matter if I took her out for a drink.'

A leading psychologist said, 'Anyone who says they've never been attracted to someone of the opposite sex after they're married is either less than human or a liar.'

He may have overstated the case, but it's natural and human to be attracted to others, and this attraction is not confined to our marriage partner. The chemistry is real and powerful – so what can we do about it?

Do you take precautions against burglars? Do you lock the doors and close the windows when you're out? Most people, very sensibly, do.

So what makes our 'house' – our marriage – an easy 'job' for burglars? What leads to the affair?

A dull marriage is one trigger. Life is so busy today. Many couples find that both have to work to pay the bills. For other couples, both want to work. The time pressure is relentless: getting the children off to school, getting to work in the rush hour, doing the garden, meetings, committees, late-night shopping...it's never ending. Also, it is often expected that employees will work long hours, and working parents get little sympathy from the boss if their children are ill or on holiday.

Keith and Wendy were married with three young children, so Wendy was at home all day. Keith came home in the evenings and dropped in front of the television. He barely spoke. He wasn't interested in Wendy's day. He wasn't interested in Wendy – or that's how it felt to her.

'I might as well have a black eye or my leg in plaster for all you care!' she yelled at him one day. But he shrugged, told her 'not to be silly', and switched on the telly.

If you are like Keith, and your wife is feeling lonely or unappreciated, watch out! Tell her she's great, spend more time with her, listen to what she's saying. She still loves you, but she didn't marry you just to be your housekeeper and childminder. She's longing for you.

'Marriages are not just made and then left to linger.' Well, some are. Keith has left his to linger, and the door is wide open for the burglar to walk in and wreck his marriage. It is an affair waiting to happen. The first man who comes into Wendy's life and gives her attention and appreciation is likely to steal her affection. Keith may still love her, but he'd better hurry up and show it, or it'll be too late.

The mid-life crisis can set off an affair. You take a fresh look at yourself. You're no longer as young, fit, slim, attractive and energetic as you once were...or that's how it feels. You're stuck in a rut, and long for something new – change, excitement. A man may suddenly feel that life and youth are passing him by. He feels the need for a 'final fling' before middle age creeps in. He wants some fun.

And it *is* fun, the affair, for a while. She's young, well turned out, hangs on every word he says, pays him

compliments and is exciting in bed. What a wonderful escape from routine! How stimulating it all is! It puts a new spring in his step and a smile on his face...for a while.

Jim said, 'At first it was terrific. Then the bills started coming in, the fridge broke down, my girlfriend "wore off" a bit, and I began to have bad dreams about the children. They were pleading with me:

"Daddy, why don't you come home? Don't you love us any more?"

"Daddy, you promised to teach me to ride my bike, remember?"

"Daddy, I miss you so. I want to hug you."

I would wake up in a sweat and think, "What have I done? What can I do?" There just seemed no way out.'

A lodger is another possible danger zone. Out of financial necessity or kindness, we take a lone man or woman into our home, and inevitably, he or she shares much of our family life with us. What starts as a straightforward arrangement can lead to increasing friendship between the lodger and the marriage partner of the opposite sex. Opportunity is there. It's all so easy – and an affair can begin so innocently.

Taking each other for granted is easy too, but it's asking for trouble. We need to *know* that we are loved and valued. We need to be *told*. If your relationship is close, if you are actively enjoying your life together, spending time with each other, expressing your love and appreciation openly, and having a good sex life, the intruder stands little chance.

But an affair can creep up on us like a burglar – unexpected, unwelcome and perhaps unprepared for. We need to guard our hearts and develop a sensitive alarm system against temptation, for it will cause tremendous pain, and possible destruction, to our family if we give in to it.

Watch Out...There's a Thief About!

Protect and Survive

How can we avoid falling into an affair? How can we protect our marriage and family, and guard against the thief who would steal our happiness?

There are a number of avoiding tactics that we can take to protect ourselves.

For example, **be open** with your spouse if you meet an attractive man or woman. My husband would come home and say, 'I met a real stunner today!', and tell me all about her. It took the kick out of it, and built trust between us.

Avoid unnecessary contact. If there is an attractive man or woman where you work, don't have coffee alone together or share lifts in each other's cars. Tempting as it may be, do your best not to be alone with them. It's better to avoid offering comfort to someone of the opposite sex. If your secretary has just been jilted by her boyfriend, find another woman to help her. If a colleague of the opposite sex is having marriage problems, beware of finding yourself in the role of the sympathetic listener. It would be much safer to get someone of their own sex to come alongside them.

Two couples were great friends and often went out together. They played games in the evenings, but one husband and the other wife liked staying up late, while the first two went off to their separate bedrooms. This was fine until one evening, the husband began to talk about his marriage problems. She listened – and it was the beginning of an affair that caused excruciating pain to two families.

Admit that it could happen to you. An affair can happen to anyone, yes, even to you, however good your marriage. If you don't believe this, you won't be on your guard, and the decisions you take in the early stages of attraction may lead you to a point when you can't pull out. The only safeguard is not to pull in.

A married man and a married woman were both members of a local drama group. They were attracted to one another, although they were both happily married with children. The group were to spend a working weekend together in Wales, and the 'couple' made arrangements to drive together in his car. That is like crossing a slippery suspension bridge without side wires in a gale-force wind. The result is just as inevitable.

Recognise the danger. There are high-voltage electricity pylons across the countryside. They have notices on them saying: 'DANGER! HIGH VOLTAGE. DO NOT TOUCH.' Chemistry is fired by touch. Beware – or the volts will start pumping through you.

The 'DANGER' notice is written large over plans such as a car journey alone, an evening meal together, yes, even the decision to leave your hand on the desk, stand next to him in the lunch queue, catch her eye and linger. Those first moments of attraction are stimulating, they're fun. You're not looking for an affair – but one thing quickly leads to another, and soon that small beginning can reach a point where it's very hard to pull back. Every affair begins with a small gesture, so small, so 'innocent', yet so dangerous.

Be aware of your own vulnerable points. If you know that your resistance is low when you're tired or feeling down, be on your guard at such times. Hurry home!

If you feel vulnerable when you are alone and lonely – and who doesn't? – be aware of that, and try to avoid attractive hazards.

A lonely wife started attending a local sports club, alone. The team coach picked her out for special praise, complimenting her on her talent. The team often had a drink together after the game. Then one day, the coach invited the lonely wife to go for another drink with him afterwards. She went.

The battle was lost in that one decision. The rest became painful history. But had she recognised the danger, she might have said, 'No'.

If pornography, in whatever form, turns you on, steer clear of it. If the girls in the office wear see-through blouses or leave off their bras, try not to look. A friend of ours says, 'You can't help the first look, but you can help the second!'

'If the grass is greener on the other side of the fence, it's time you watered your own.' Grass can't survive without water. Get out the sprinkler now. Greet each other with real warmth and pleasure. Sit down, even if you've only got five minutes, and listen with genuine interest to your partner as you talk about the day. Share some happy moment or a difficulty that arose, hold hands, show that you care, have a hug or a cuddle. These are the little things that keep our own grass greener.

After all, how can I know that my husband loves me if he never listens to me, never sits down to talk with me, never does things with me? How can I know my wife is pleased to have me home if she just carries on putting the children to bed or cooking the tea without so much as a look or a word in my direction?

Have a surprise sometimes! It gets you out of the rut and stops the rot.

Clive got a rise, and decided to take his wife on a day trip to Paris on 'Le Shuttle'.

Debbie planned a surprise party for Adam's fortieth birthday, inviting lots of his old friends.

Ian came home one day with a pretty silver ring for his wife. 'Just because I love you,' he said.

What surprises can you think of that would give your partner real pleasure? They're such fun to plan, and bring a sparkle into our lives. They guard against dullness.

The costly affair. There is hardly ever an affair

where the couple 'live happily ever after'. Within a year or two, many bitterly regret what they've done, and long to put the clock back.

A typical comment was Barry's: 'I had a super wife, two smashing kids and a nice home, and I've lost the lot. I wish I could start again.' The excitement had worn off, he was filled with shame and guilt, he missed the kids so much, but it was too late.

Before we are ever tempted into an affair, this is the time to count the cost if it ever happened. Dare to discuss it together, and then make a pact that you'll always tell each other if you meet anyone attractive, and you'll never get involved with them.

Talk through what it would do to you both, and the terrible, life-long damage it would inflict on the children. See the temptation for what it is – sugar-coated dynamite, that would blow your hearts and lives to pieces. Determine that you will look after your marriage. See the 'affair' for the betrayal of trust that it is.

Look behind the glamour at the broken lives it causes – and decide against it now.

If you are reading this, and are already on the slippery slope, pause a minute. Think what you're doing. Think where it will lead. Think what it will do to those you love. Think what you stand to lose. And step back before it's too late. It'll be hard, very hard, but the way forward will be much harder in the end.

What it it's happened to me? And if it's happened already, there's only one way back; real sorrow, deep, deep regret, understanding the enormity of what you've done. Confess it, perhaps to a church minister or a counsellor, and ask forgiveness. You have betrayed those who loved and trusted you. You have caused terrible hurt and pain. You need to take full responsibility for what has happened, make no excuses, don't blame your spouse, but humbly ask forgiveness.

The offended partner may be very angry, which means they are deeply hurt, which in turn means they still love you very much. You must accept that, and give them time to recover from the shock and the pain.

Jack went to his vicar. He couldn't stand his conscience and the deceit of his life any more. He was having an affair that he'd managed to keep from his wife for a year, but he'd had enough. Confessing it all, he wept and wept, and wondered how he could ever tell June.

The following week, Jack and June came together, and with the vicar there, he told her as gently as he could. She was distraught. She sobbed and sobbed, and for days afterwards she kept asking him questions. 'Where did you go?' 'When did it start?' 'How often have you been meeting?'

It was so hard for her, and Jack felt so miserable. It took months before June was fully able to forgive him, and they could start rebuilding their marriage. Slowly, she learned to trust him again, and now their marriage is stronger than it was before the affair, but they wouldn't recommend their experience to anyone.

In the pressures of today's world, the affair is only one step round the corner. Sex shouts at us from the rooftops. Adultery and divorce no longer carry the shame they once did. Opportunities abound. Cash, cars and commuting, trips abroad, motels – all make it so easy.

The condom is safe against Aids, they say – but it isn't. The failure rate is alarmingly high.

The pill has removed the fear of pregnancy – nearly.

The media glorify casual affairs and sex, and dishonour marriage.

How can we resist all this, and stay faithful to one another as we promised when we married? We were asked on that day: 'Will you take John/Jill to be your husband/wife? Will you *love* him/her, *comfort* him/her, *honour* and *protect* him/her, and, *forsaking* all others, be *faithful to him/her as long as you both shall live?*' The question was put to each of you, and each of you answered: *'I will.'*

You chose to make those promises. Nobody made you do it. You did it freely. 'I will,' you promised, and meant it. *Will you?* It's the only path to true happiness.

Take stock of your defences against any instrusions in your relationship. Talk it through with your partner.

The Original Design

R ichard and Mary set off in their car to drive home from Wales to southern England.

'Let's go by a more interesting route,' suggested Richard. 'We've seen enough of motorways.'

'Fine,' said Mary. 'I'll have a look at the road atlas.'

'No, don't bother,' said Richard. 'We know the way well enough.' So they set off, but after a while, the roads got very narrow, until finally, they ended up with a farm gate across the road.

'Do you think we might find it useful to look at the map?' said Mary quietly.

'If you want to, I suppose,' agreed Richard grudgingly. After a good look at it and a lot of back-tracking, they eventually found their way onto a proper road again.

Jeanette bought a microwave. All her friends had told her what a useful machine it was, and she found one with 20% off in the sales, so she took the plunge.

It came with a recipe book and instruction manual, but she couldn't be bothered with those. She just remembered everyone said it was quick, so she put some soup in, without a lid, and set the microwave on full power for ten minutes. After five minutes, she noticed some liquid coming out under the door of the oven. The soup had boiled up over the top of the jug and was pouring out everywhere.

'Bother!' Jeanette said aloud. 'I'd better check the book next time.'

Janie decided to wash her jeans and shirts, saw some whites on the top of the washing machine, so threw them in too. She took no notice of the little label on her dark tops that said: 'Wash dark colours separately.'

When she came to get them out, all the whites were a murky shade of blue/black.

We've all done it. Ignored the road atlas, instruction manual or cookery book, and had disasters of one sort or another. The designer, whether of videos, microwaves or anything else, knows exactly how the machine works and how to get the best results from using it. We ignore the instructions at our peril – and often render the guarantee void in the process.

Marriage has a designer too. He first created the world, then as the climax of all that he had made, he created a man and a woman. He gave them to each other one glorious day in a beautiful garden – you may call it Eden if you like – and the first marriage began.

At that stage in history, there was no wrong in the world at all. The designer, God, himself perfectly loving and a brilliant creator, checked that everything that he had made was very good, and union between a man and woman was no exception. It was very good. There was no fault in the design. The partnership was intended to bring total fulfilment and joy.

When the man and the woman met, they were thrilled and fascinated with each other. They soon discovered how different they were, yet how wonderfully complementary. They seemed to 'fit' each other and to suit one another so well. They found each other such good company. They laughed together as they splashed in the river, sat munching delicious fruit in the shade of the trees, and made love in the cool of the evening.

Made to measure. God invented marriage, and he has never needed to change the original design. The instructions that came with it are unaltered since creation, and when they are followed, the results are still good.

It is we who have proudly presumed we know better, and invented other rules, or thrown them away altogether, and in our selfishness, have spoiled its riches. So let's have a look at the original design.

First of all, God made male and female, one man, one woman. Just think how dull the world would be if we were all the same! It would be as colourless as a garden in a fog – all grey.

Creation was not complete until the woman was made. God made man and woman alike in some ways, yet with fundamental differences that give marriage the potential of a richness beyond compare. We are designed so that we find it intriguing and challenging to get to know each other.

The man was lonely, and God saw that it was 'not good'. He needed a companion, so he united him with the best woman in the world – and true happiness was born. There was literally nothing in the world to spoil their relationship or their joy.

Our instinctive desire in life is to share with someone who really cares, both the major events and the everyday details of our lives. We long to pass on good news, tell of the successful game, moan about the weather, seek help over a cut finger, rejoice over a family event – and marriage gives us that opportunity. It was woven into the fabric by the designer from the very beginning.

Love is ...

Love is inexhaustibly patient.

Love anticipates a person's needs and meets them.

Love doesn't mind when someone else has the limelight, responsibilities, popularity or privileges.

Love is not anxious to impress.

Love does not blow its own trumpet.

Love is not aggressive, but courteous.

Love does not insist on its own way.

Love is not touchy, or easily rubbed up the wrong way.

Love keeps no list of the faults and failings of others.

Love doesn't gloat over the mistakes of others in order to put itself in a better light; instead it is glad when others are right.

Love throws a cloak of silence over what is displeasing in other people.

Love trusts that in everything God works for good.

Love is not shaken even by the worst of storms.

Love is eternal.

(Part of a translation of 1 Corinthians 13:4 – 8a
by Canon David Watson)

The designer marriage. He intended marriage to be a loving, life-long commitment. Even today, this is what most people want. The *Times* newspaper commented in July 1994: 'Marriage maintains its allure. Britons are still eager to marry despite having the highest divorce rate in Europe.' A recent survey on marriage revealed that 'people are simply not content with possible alternatives such as casual affairs'. The survey speaks of people's 'profound and intense longing for a permanent relationship', and found that most couples living together are not satisfied with the unmarried state.

The designer has given us three very important instructions for marriage. The first is that we **leave** all other relationships when we marry, and make our marriage the primary commitment of our life. This doesn't mean that we lose touch with our family and friends, but it does mean that the first priority for our love and loyalty is our spouse from now on.

The second instruction is to **cleave** to one another, which simply means to stick like glue, in good times and bad. If both partners determine to do this, it brings great confidence and security into the relationship. Without this there cannot be real happiness.

The third instruction is that we become **one flesh.** This is a far wider term than physical union, although this in itself is one of God's greatest gifts to us. If we are relating in a really loving way, the pleasure, excitement and satisfaction that we can experience in making love, must be one of the designer's best inspirations. Brilliant! Who could have invented anything so wonderful and so delightful? Only God himself. At its best, it is the full expression of our wider union.

However, the full meaning of our becoming 'one flesh' is far better than this. It speaks of our growing into a deep intimacy with one another, and knowing each other's hearts and minds, emotions and thoughts. It involves sharing more and more of our innermost self with one another, entering into the secret places that no one else is ever allowed to share.

A couple who have truly left their earlier emotional ties, are cleaving together through the good and the tough times, and are entering into an ever-deepening intimacy at all levels of their relationship, are likely to be enjoying the delights that come from following the maker's instructions.

Many alternatives to the original design have been tried, but none has brought happiness. The tragic consequences of every other option are all around us.

Your marriage can become happier and more satisfying year by year as you work through the various areas that need attention. If you want the very best, seek the help of the designer, and start following his instructions.

Marriage is a most treasured, precious relationship. Give it your best, and you will gain the best.

What's important to you?

Here's a questionnaire to help you and your partner understand each other, and to get you talking! Simply look at the list and put a tick in the appropriate column to show how important each aspect is to you. Then go through it again and mark where your partner stands. Finally, compare notes!

	Your Answers ☐		Your Partner's ○	
	VERY		**NOT VERY**	
My job	☐	○	☐	○
Having a nice house	☐	○	☐	○
Being tidy and well-organised	☐	○	☐	○
Being punctual	☐	○	☐	○
Inviting people round	☐	○	☐	○
Having my own friends	☐	○	☐	○
Family ties	☐	○	☐	○
Regular evenings out	☐	○	☐	○
Hobbies	☐	○	☐	○
Reading	☐	○	☐	○
Watching TV	☐	○	☐	○
Having time to myself	☐	○	☐	○
Going to church	☐	○	☐	○
Working to an agreed budget	☐	○	☐	○
Saving	☐	○	☐	○
Taking care over decisions	☐	○	☐	○
Talking together	☐	○	☐	○
Keeping promises	☐	○	☐	○
Keeping the peace	☐	○	☐	○
Getting my own way	☐	○	☐	○
Showing affection	☐	○	☐	○
Saying 'I love you'	☐	○	☐	○
Love making	☐	○	☐	○

Think of some other things which are important issues affecting you.

Adapted and used with permission from *Woman Alive Magazine*.

More Ideas

BOOKS

Willard F. Harley, *His Needs, Her Needs* (Monarch Publications, 1994), ISBN 1-85424-274-1.

Christina Hughes, *Step-parents, Step-children* (Kyle Cathie, 1993), ISBN 1-85626-082-8.

Sarah Litvinoff, *The Relate Guide to Better Relationships* (Vermillion, 1993), ISBN 0-09-177432-2.

Sarah Litvinoff, *The Relate Guide to Sex in Loving Relationships* (Vermillion, 1992), ISBN 0-09-175294-9.

Sarah Litvinoff, *The Relate Guide to Starting Again* (Vermillion, 1993), ISBN 0-09-175295-7.

Rob Parsons, *Loving Against the Odds* (Hodder Headlines, 1994), ISBN 0-340-59315-6.

Dr Trevor Stammers, *The Family Guide to Sex and Intimacy* (Hodder Headlines, 1994), ISBN 0-340-60816-1.

Keith Tondeur, *Escape from Debt* (Credit Action, 1993).

There are a wealth of other helpful books available from Christian and general Bookshops. Check your local directory for details.

VIDEOS

Marriage Matters
Part 1 –   Communication and Time Pressure.

Resolving Conflict. Appreciation.

Loving Against the Odds.

Part 2 –   Sex in Marriage.

Men and the Affair.

Expectations and Realities.

The Adam and Eve Factor
1. Commitment.
2. Conflict.
3. Intimacy.
4. Servanthood.

Obtainable from SP/Valley Trust Ltd, Triangle Business Park, Wendover Road, Stoke Mandeville, Aylesbury, Bucks, HP22 5BL England. Tel: (01296) 614430

Beating Burn-out

How to survive in a stress-filled world.

Obtainable from Care for the Family, 136 Newport Road, Cardiff CF2 1DJ Tel: 01222 494431 Fax: 01222 497807.

Time for Each Other

1. Understanding Each Other.
2. Equal but Different.
3. Let's be Friends.
4. Let's Communicate.
5. Giving Love or Getting Sex?

Obtainable from Family College, King's House, 175 Wokingham Road, Reading, RG6 1LU. Tel. 01734 660010.

Staying Together

Deals with marital and family pressures.

Obtainable from Family and Youth Concern, Wicken, Milton Keynes, MK19 6BU. Tel. 01908 57234.

Marriage – What it Takes

1. Communication.
2. Commitment.
3. Conflict.

Obtainable from St. Pauls, Morpeth Terrace, Victoria, London SW1 1EP. Tel. 0171 828 5582.

MARRIAGE SEMINARS

Rapport (one-day seminars)

Workshops on Marriage –	'Communication'.
	'Growing Together'.
Workshops on the Family –	'Parenting Children'.
	'Parenting Teenagers'.

Details from Rapport, Charnwood House, 2A Forest Road, Loughborough, LE11 3NP. Tel. 01509 212808.

Marriage Encounter (Residential weekend seminars)
Details from David and Liz Percival, 11 Lambourne Close, Sandhurst,
Berks. GU47 8JL Tel: 01344 779658.

Engaged Encounter (Residential weekend seminars)
Details from Derek and Judy Hunt, 38 Pennine Way, Ashby de la
Zouche, Leicestershire, LE6 5EW. Tel. 01530 413005.

Association for Marriage Enrichment
(Residential or local workshops)
Details from David and Judith Robinson, 67 Between Streets,
Cobham, Surrey, KT11 1AA. Tel. 01932 862090.

COUNSELLING

Marriage Resource
PO Box 2316, Wimborne, Dorset, BH21 1FD. Tel. 01202 849433.

Care for the Family
Write or ring *Care for the Family*, 136 Newport Road, Cardiff
CF2 1DJ   Tel: 01222 494431   Fax: 01222 497807.

Relate
Counselling for Adult couples facing difficulties in their relationship.

London
Inner London Marriage Guidance.

Scotland
Marriage Counselling Scotland. Refer to direction's for local area or
consult your Citizens' Advice Bureaux.

For further details or help:
Write or ring *Care for the Family*, 136 Newport Road, Cardiff
CF2 1DJ Tel: 01222 494431   Fax: 01222 497807 who will be very
pleased to assist in any way they can.